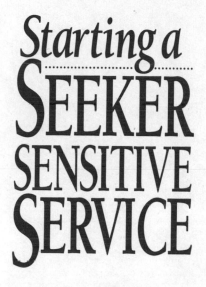

Starting a
SEEKER
SENSITIVE
SERVICE

Starting a SEEKER SENSITIVE SERVICE

HOW TRADITIONAL CHURCHES CAN REACH THE UNCHURCHED

Ed Dobson

ZondervanPublishingHouse
Academic and Professional Books
Grand Rapids, Michigan

A Division of HarperCollinsPublishers

Requests for information should be addressed to:
Zondervan Publishing House
Academic and Professional Books
Grand Rapids, Michigan 49530

People mentioned in testimonies and other portions of this book have granted permission to be quoted and to be identified by their actual names. Some testimonies have been edited for length.

The abbreviation NIV refers to the HOLY BIBLE: NEW INTERNATIONAL VERSION® (North American Edition). Copyright © 1973, 1978, 1984, by the International Bible Society.

Cover design by Terry Dugan Design
Cover photos by Mike Carter
Edited by James E. Ruark

Library of Congress Cataloging-in-Publication Data
Dobson, Ed.
    Starting a seeker-sensitive service : how traditional churches can reach the unchurched / Ed Dobson
        p.   cm.
    ISBN 0-310-38481-8
    1. Evangelistic work—Michigan—Grand Rapids—History—20th century. 2. Calvary Church (Grand Rapids, Mich.) 3.Dobson, Ed. 4. Non-church-affiliated people—United States—Religious life. I. Title. II. Title: Seeker-sensitive service.
BV3775.G73D62   1993   93-19863
269'.2—dc20   CIP

Printed in the United States of America

93 94 95 96 97 / DH / 9 8 7 6 5 4 3 2 1

CONTENTS

5)

PREFACE

*T*his is a book about radical change. It is the story of how a traditional church launched a nontraditional service in order to open its doors to unchurched people. This book has grown out of five years of ministry to hurting people who are either skeptics, agnostics, or doubters of the Christian faith. It has been shaped by people who do not give much of a rip about God or the Bible, but they are at least willing to listen. It is a book about what I have learned from these fellow travelers in the adventure of life.

As the senior pastor of Calvary Church I became concerned that our ministry was not reaching unchurched people. We were reaching many people from religious backgrounds, but not many hard-core skeptics. I asked several friends to join me in exploring how we could start a ministry that would be geared to the needs of people who have lived outside religious circles. We spent nearly a year reading, researching, and deciding what we should do.

What happened? Five years ago we began a service on Saturday night that we called "Saturday Night—A Place to Answer Questions." The format is non- (almost anti-) traditional. The music is contemporary rock and roll. We use drama. The dress code is blue jeans and T-shirts. The format is informal. I give a talk (sermon) while sitting on a bar stool (renamed a church stool), and at the end of the talk I receive written questions from the audience. That is—and is not—about all there is to it.

I am deeply indebted to the men and women who shared the initial vision for this endeavor. I wish to thank the board and congregation of Calvary Chruch for their tolerance, prayers, and support in developing our seeker-sensitive service. I wish to thank the ministry staff and volunteers who make "Saturday Night" happen every week. Last, I wish to thank the hundreds of unchurched people whose questions, struggles, and lives have deeply affected and changed me. It has been an incredible journey—and it has only begun.

—ED DOBSON
Calvary Church
Grand Rapids, Michigan

Starting a
SEEKER
SENSITIVE
SERVICE

I had been searching for "something more" ever since I could remember. My searching led me to Southern California—land of opportunity, sunshine, the Golden State. That's the way it's supposed to be anyway. What I found was rude people, lots of traffic, a smog-filled sky, and lots of loneliness. So I started talking to God.

I'd always believed in God and accepted Jesus as my Savior when I was twenty. But it never went from my head to my heart. During the next ten years God was aways putting Christians in my life, knowing someday I'd hear him knocking—and I did. I invited Jesus into my life again in June 1992 and I meant it this time. And I knew he heard me because a beautiful butterfly landed on my shoulder and stayed there for a few minutes. We (God and I) decided it would be best for me to move back to Grand Rapids. When I got back, some friends told me about "Saturday Night" at Calvary. So I checked it out, and what I found was *wonderful!* Through "Saturday Night" I've been plugged into a great Bible study, a Sunday school class, and traditional services on Sunday. I've met many Christian friends, and my faith has grown tremendously.

I really feel God is using "Saturday Night" as a vehicle to reach my generation, those searching and those who maybe wouldn't make an effort to attend traditional services. As for me, I'm sure that without "Saturday Night," my Christian walk would still be on the porch!

—*Craig Nelson*

CHAPTER 1

STARTING A SEEKER-SENSITIVE SERVICE

I t was an unforgettable moment. I was sitting on the bar stool in my blue jeans and sweatshirt. I had just finished my "Saturday Night" talk on the subject "Forgiving Your Parents," and I was in the middle of the question-answer time. I looked at the next question card, and it was typewritten. *Somebody brought this question with him or her,* I thought. *It must be important.* I read the question: "My mother died when I was young. And my dad remarried. He married a bitch. My greatest joy in life will be when she dies and I stand at her grave and sing the Doxology."

I read the question aloud as it was written—the word *bitch* and all. When I finished, there was a nervous rumble of laughter from some people in the audience. I had hardly begun my response when the person who had written the question spoke up. "That was *my* question," he said, interrupting me, "and I don't appreciate people laughing at me. I'm going through hell and it's not funny!" Suddenly there was absolute silence. No one, including me, knew quite what to do.

I looked this young man in the eye and began a ten-minute conversation with him. I apologized for those who laughed. I talked about the idea of forgiving and what that meant for his situation. The conversation seemed like an eternity. When the program was over, a long line of people formed to talk to this man and hug him. I waited until everyone else had talked to him and then I hugged him, thanked him for his honesty, and told him I loved him.

The next week I received a letter from the same man, whose name is David. He told of a painful childhood, religious abuse, and his lifelong struggle with cerebral palsy. He told me that the traditional church was a joke. He said he doubted life has any meaning or purpose. At the end of the letter he said that "Saturday Night" was the *only* church service he ever attended where he felt loved and accepted—the only service where he felt the sermons were honest. This was amazing, for David had graduated from a theological seminary.

David continued to attend "Saturday Night." He found new faith in Christ. Sometime later, he stood before the "Saturday Night" crowd and shared what God was doing in his life. I was thrilled. I fought back the tears as he declared how his faith in God was sustaining him through his continuing daily struggles.

David would not and does not attend the traditional services at Calvary Church. Without a seeker-sensitive service, our ministry would not have touched David. Why do we do "Saturday Night"? Because of the Davids in our community: people who feel life has no meaning or purpose, who have rejected traditional religion but are open to God and the Bible. In five years of ministry on Saturday night the unchurched people have come by the hundreds. The pain and struggle of these people is reflected in a dramatic way by the questions they ask. These questions are not typical "church" questions; they embody the issues of everyday living. I have looked through hundreds of these written questions, and this is a representative sampling:

- I don't care about God giving me a second chance. I want to know where your God was when I was 2, 3, 4, 5, 6, 7, 8, 9, 10, 11, 12 and I was sexually and physically abused. Why should I give God a second chance?
- I'm gay. Is that okay?
- How can I know for sure that God is a reality and not just a psychological crutch?
- Why couldn't you go past 7:00 p.m. to try to answer a few more questions?

- It used to be that you knew someone liked you if they had sex with you. Nowadays sex is like shaking hands. So how do you know whether someone likes you?

- Open meetings in an open society take oral questions from the floor. You give the impression you want to control the questions, which makes your intellectual arguments seem dishonest. Would you shift to an open format of oral questions?

- How do you overcome fears and walls formed from past hurts? How does one let go of fear and begin to trust? Why does God often limit himself to humans?

- How can I love someone who hurts me?

- How do you honestly break up a long-term relationship because you are not in love with the other person?

- Do you think Buddhism, Hinduism, and Islam, etc., are a front for the devil?

- I dip my forefinger in the watery blood of your impotent redeemer. I write above his thorn-torn brow, "The TRUE prince of evil—King of the Slaves. Satanic Bible, Book of Satan."

- Why is it that people dress up for church on Sundays, but not Saturdays? I realize this is an informal service, but what is the difference?

- If someone asks you to tell them the honest truth and you know the truth will hurt, what do you do?

- What if the burden or difficulty someone is facing is harmful to others and after continual prayer to take it away it is still hurting people?

- Does God punish us with trials and tribulations?

- Is it wrong to have sex before marriage if you're engaged? If so, why?

Why a Seeker-Sensitive Service?

There is no question that the Willow Creek Community Church has radically challenged the thinking of traditional churches. The church in South Barrington, Illinois, offers a model of ministry that is "consumer" oriented. It attempts to relate the gospel in a culturally relevant way to un-churched men and women. And judging by the thousands who attend, the church has achieved unique results. People flock to its seminars, buy its materials, and emulate its model. Why? Why develop ministry based on this model? I continually examine my own motives in our ongoing endeavor to be seeker sensitive on Saturday nights. Several compelling reasons have emerged from my efforts to understand why.

1. *We are trapped in an evangelical subculture.* As evangelical Christians we are isolated in our own *little* world. That world is basically out of touch with the broader culture. We have our own heroes, books, media, music, language, educational institutions, and taboos.

Heroes: James Kennedy, Charles Stanley, Elisabeth Elliot, James Dobson, Chuck Swindoll
Books: Zondervan, Baker, Eerdmans, Word, Thomas Nelson, Moody
Media: Televangelism, radio, *Christianity Today, Moody Monthly,* TBN, CBN
Language: "Exegetical," "born again," "reformed," "dispensational," "anointed"
Taboos: Guys with ponytails and/or earrings, dancing, nuclear disarmament, simplicity

All these add up to a language and culture understood by, defended to, and passed on for another generation of evangelicals. It also removes evangelicalism further from the unchurched community. Nonevangelicals have never heard of our heroes, read our books, tuned in to our television and radio programs, bought our music, or given a second thought to our taboos.

Recently Larnelle Harris, a Christian recording artist, came to Grand Rapids for a concert on a Saturday night. The concert was to be held at another church, and the Calvary Church choir was asked to back him up. The event had a big draw—sold out. Before that weekend I was nervous that the concert would affect attendance at our regular "Saturday Night" event. I figured that half the crowd would skip our service and go to hear Larnelle.

I was wrong. Our attendance on the night of the concert was actually higher than usual! Why? Because seventy percent of the people who attend "Saturday Night" are unchurched and they have very likely never heard of Larnelle Harris. Their cultural point of reference is radically different from mine.

As I write, I am on a plane on one leg of a trip to Poland. On the flight out of Grand Rapids I was sitting across from D. James Kennedy. I followed him and his entourage through the Cincinnati airport, and I was amazed that no one seemed to recognize him even though he is on national television. Most Christians would recognize him as a hero in our evangelical subculture—but in the larger culture he moves about with relative anonymity. "Business as usual" in the church will not reach those in the larger culture who do not know the Lord. "Business as usual" is simply preaching to the choir. It is passing along our culture to the next generation without spreading the boundaries. To reach the nonevangelical generation of our day, we must break out of our tradition-bound isolation and relate the gospel to people where they are.

2. *We are missionaries in a foreign land.* Because we are trapped in an evangelical subculture, we must understand the larger culture and use its language to communicate Christ. We understand this principle when we send missionaries to other countries. These missionaries seek first to learn the language and the culture of the places to which they go. Only then do they attempt to communicate the gospel.

We would never send an English-speaking missionary to a Spanish-speaking county to minister exclusively in English. That would be irrational, not to mention stupid. Yet we continue to preach the gospel in the United States in evangelical language to a skeptical, secular-speaking audience. And the tragedy is that they don't understand what we are saying, and we don't understand that our message is couched in a foreign language.

Years ago I did a lot of speaking for an organization called Word of Life. They conducted all-day Saturday basketball marathons in major cities around the country. In the middle of the competition they would have all the players sit on the floor and would introduce me to speak to them about Jesus Christ. No music. No drama. No entertainment. Just thirty minutes of talk with sweaty ballplayers in a gymnasium.

I remember one marathon in Baltimore. More than 1,500 players attended, most of them unchurched youths from the inner city. More than 300 came forward to receive Christ. Word of Life had learned that the language of high school inner-city youth was basketball. So they spoke the language to get their attention and to point them to Christ. Word of Life put the gospel in a context and a culture that was relevant to these kids.

It is not a long way from basketball to rock music, drama, and the good news about Jesus Christ. A seeker-sensitive service is an attempt to place the gospel in a culturally relevant context. The language of contemporary music, drama that engages, talks that are relevant, and answers that are honest make up the language of secular America. Just as the gospel was not compromised at a basketball marathon, neither is it compromised in a seeker-sensitive service.

Getting Started

I am frequently asked about starting a seeker-sensitive service. "Tell me what I need to get going," people say. Obviously there are many factors at work to get a service going in a traditional setting, but there is one compelling issue. There is a tendency to overlook this matter as not all that important. To me it is the ultimate issue, and I introduce it in the form of a question: Do I have a consuming passion for the evangelism of the unchurched?

You have probably already answered "yes" and shrugged off the point as obvious and insubstantial. But hold on. I want to tell a story.

Several years ago I was invited to speak at the annual Founder's Week celebration at Moody Bible Institute. I sat at dinner one evening with Dr. Joseph Stowell (the president of Moody) and his wife, some other speakers, and several members of the faculty. The conversation turned to what Calvary Church is doing on Saturday nights. After some discussion, Dr. Stowell asked what advice I would give to pastors who want to start a nontraditional service. I described the following hypothetical situation:

"Suppose you were asked to speak tonight at Founder's Week. You would teach the Bible to four thousand-plus people at Moody Church, and you would be heard live on radio all over the country. Or you had the chance to meet with twenty nonbelieving skeptics to talk about Jesus Christ in an open forum. Which choice would you make?

"If you would choose to speak at Founder's Week or you even lean in that direction, don't start a seeker service, because you will fail. But if your immediate, enthusiastic choice is twenty skeptics—if that excites you beyond description—then go ahead with a seeker-sensitive service. Your passion is evangelism."

There are other ways to address your passion. If you don't like people blowing smoke in your face or drinking in front of you, if you don't like to be the only Christian surrounded by pagans, if you can't stand being around cursing, if, if, if—then stay in the evangelical subculture where you will be safe. Once in a while a lost person will stumble into your fold. Great! But if your passion is to love, accept, and meet people on their turf, and if your passion is evangelism, then you are a good candidate to lead seeker-sensitive services.

When we reach people where they are and they make a commitment to Jesus Christ, they will probably not fit the traditional understanding of the Christian faith. They will say and do things that will shatter traditionalism. They may show up on Sunday and make everyone else uncomfortable.

I remember one such person who, on the way out of a Sunday morning service, declared loud enough for several dozen to hear, "That was one hell of a service!" Another person showed up on Sunday morning wearing a T-shirt with the "F" word on it. If you don't want these kinds of people in the church, don't start a service for unchurched people.

Don't start a seeker-sensitive service to get more people inside the church. Don't start a seeker-sensitive service because you feel a need to change. Don't start a seeker-sensitive service because Willow Creek does it. Don't start a seeker-sensitive service because it is the "in" thing to do. Don't start a seeker-sensitive service because people in the church want you to do it. Don't start a seeker-sensitive service because you would like to do it. Start a seeker-sensitive service because you have a personal and all-consuming passion for people who don't know the Lord. If that passion is not there and real, then the service will fail because your heart is not in it. And unchurched people will be the first to pick up on your uneasiness with them and will dismiss you as the typical "Christian" hypocrite.

Honest Self-Evaluation

The problem with evangelism today is that nearly every Christian is agreeable to it, but very few are practicing it. For me, starting a seeker-sensitive service was another logical step in a ministry-long pilgrimage in evangelism. I did evangelism before we started "Saturday Night." If we had not started the service, I would still be doing evangelism in some form.

My first pastoral experience was in starting a Baptist church in the mountain town of Buena Vista, Virginia. We started with thirty-three people and baptized more than two hundred converts in less than two years. I went door to door sharing Christ. I followed up with home visits to the people who visited the church. We ran Sunday school contests: water gun Sunday, balloon Sunday, kite Sunday, and so on. I even preached from the roof of a building one Sunday.

(That was twenty years ago; simply mentioning it now is embarrassing.) The point of all these promotions was evangelism, and through them many unchurched people came to know Christ.

Twenty years later, we don't give out water guns or balloons. But we do use drama. We don't go door to door, but we run "rap" commercials on the local "Oldies" radio station. I don't preach from the rooftop (it's too sensational), but I do sit on a bar stool while dressed in blue jeans and a sweatshirt. The times have changed. The culture has changed. The methods have changed. But the motive remains the same: using every available means to reach every available person with the gospel.

The seeker-sensitive service is not the only evangelistic endeavor at Calvary Church. We have Christmas and Easter programs intended for evangelism. We conduct divorce recovery workshops, Bible studies, youth outreaches, and many other programs that are designed to share the gospel in a culturally relevant way. While "Saturday Night" is the most visible by the standards of a traditional church, it is only one of the many ways we do evangelism.

Bottom-Line Questions

The primary requirement for developing a seeker-sensitive service is a passion for evangelism. I am afraid that this passion is too often lost in seminary training or absorbed by the expectations of the traditional evangelical subculture. In either case, most pastors and church lay leaders are more committed to maintaining the status quo than departing from it to reach people who would not be reached otherwise.

Do you have a passion for unchurched people? Do you attempt to understand where they are? Do you get excited about sharing Christ with the unchurched? One way to deal with these questions is to look over the following questions that were all submitted in just one "Saturday Night." The topic for the evening was human sexuality and the Bible. Responding to questions like these forces me to move from safe ground into the uncharted territory of the unchurched.

If these questions intimidate or threaten you, be careful about starting a seeker-sensitive service—or ask God to help you become seeker-sensitive.

- Can you give some practical advice on how to stop sexual activity in a relationship without ending the closeness that has developed? We are a mature Christian couple and spend a lot of time alone with each other. How can we go back to a non-sexual relationship after going so far? I'm scared that God will judge us, since we both feel it's wrong and try to stop, but can't. We don't have actual intercourse, but feel uncomfortable with how far we do go.
- What would you say is too far when you are engaged to be married?
- For any of you out there who have been sexually involved or are thinking of it as a single person, please listen. I know the guilt and heartache it can bring. I am living proof that God forgives and He can bring happiness in life as a single without sex. You can say "No" with His help even after you've sinned and gone against His will.
- Someone I love very much is outside of God's "guidelines" of sexual conduct. Do I have a responsibility in any way to confront this person?
- How should we, as Christians, react to or deal with the explicit sexual content portrayed in Madonna's videos, TV, etc.?
- Sex means nothing to me. I don't regret what I have done, just the outcome. All I want is someone to hold me and be there when I need them. Why can't I find a girl like this? A friend once told me I was looking in the wrong gender.
- Why is it so difficult for parents and children to discuss such an important topic as sex?
- Being a child of God and a sex addict, I wonder where does our God come in when we fall short? Spiritually I know the truth; could you tell me in the New Testament why should we find truth?
- How often does God forgive us for adultery?

- I believe that sex belongs within a marital relationship. How can I convince those whom I date? It seems that's all they push for. Eventually the relationship ends, and that is painful. (We've been married before; I know the difference.) Could you address the differences in the Old Testament and New Testament multiple-wife arrangements? Were these marriages blessed by God?
- I was sexually abused in a previous relationship. I'm now remarried. I'm having trouble trusting my husband not to hurt me. I'm dealing with a lot of bad memories. What now?
- Does the gift of celibacy for the priesthood mean the absence of sexual desire and a non-interest in female companionship is present—or does it mean a greater discipline in the practice of self-control and denial?
- Okay, I'm a Christian and I agree with you about marriage. Thank God! But I'm a single guy, 21 years old, a committed Christian, and I am very attracted (normally) to women, yet I read in Scripture to be pure. In my dating and everyday experience, how specifically can I remain *pure?* What are the appropriate guidelines?
- Are homosexuals living outside God's boundaries when living in a monogamous relationship?
- Is masturbation a sin?
- Thank you for this service!

My name is Philip Arena. Until three months ago I spent most of my life in New York City. I was raised in a Catholic home and attended Catholic schools. At the age of fourteen I broke completely away from the church. I pursued my own interests and wants. In my senior year of high school I started smoking pot. I had already been drinking since I was thirteen. The pot led to "speed" and coke and barbiturates. I attended college for a year, and then I decided to open my own business. So a friend and I opened a pizzeria.

We worked very hard and built one store into three stores. By the time I was twenty-four I was earning $300,000 a year. My drugging and drinking kept increasing. I found my health failing and my interest in work failing. So I sold out my share of the stores for $750,000.

I took most of that money and went to Europe for a while, where I spent all of the money on drugs, alcohol, and all the madness that it offers. I came back broke and very sick. I tried to straighten out for a while and got a good job with a railroad company. Then I started up again, this time on crack-cocaine.

That was the end. I ended up losing my job, losing my house. I started to go to dangerous crack houses in the South Bronx. I suffered a heart attack from a crack and heroin overdose.

When I was in the hospital a second time, a Christian couple I knew told me about the Bowery Mission Discipleship Program. I had nowhere to go after I was released, so I went to the Mission. It was there I learned about the lordship of Christ and his plan for my life. I am now happy and healthy and pursuing his lead. In Jesus' name,

—*Philip Arena*

CHAPTER 2

IN THE BEGINNING

I am not exactly sure when the idea of a seeker-sensitive service developed in my thinking. When I became pastor of Calvary Church in March 1987, I did not have such a service on my agenda. There were, however, several factors that influenced my thinking.

First, I am a former "youth evangelist." For most of my years of ministry I spoke to junior high and senior high students and young adults. I spoke at youth camps, athletic events, youth revivals, single-adult events, and college chapels. Many of these settings were "nontraditional." I was particularly impressed with Kansas City Youth For Christ, where I had spoken many times. They still hold a weekly rally on Saturday nights that is attended by more than 2,000 teenagers. When I came to Grand Rapids I had a desire to start something in the community similar to the old Youth For Christ Rally.

Second, I had read numerous articles about Bill Hybels and Willow Creek Community Church. I obtained a video of one of their services. I remember the day I viewed the video in my office. I was alone. I had been thinking about an innovative service, and I put the tape in the machine with anticipation. I was not prepared for the music. After listening to the "prelude" played by the band, I thought, *If I do this in Calvary Church I will be thrown out on my ear.*

Don't get me wrong: I *like* the music. After all, I grew up in the late sixties. But I knew that this style would offend and shock the tastes of anyone aged forty-five or over (that is, the leadership of Calvary Church). I became discouraged, but I pressed on.

Third, I considered the explosive growth we were encountering on Sunday morning. We soon packed the sanctuary (2,000) and in the fall of 1987 added a second morning worship service. Our attendance grew by about 500 in 1987, 1988, and 1989. But I was troubled by the growth: A significant portion was composed of Christians from other churches. They enjoyed our worship experience and the verse-by-verse Bible exposition that characterizes my preaching. They were white, upper-middle-class evangelicals. Although some other kinds of people were getting converted, most of the growth consisted of just more of what we already had.

I longed to reach beyond the evangelical community. I felt that the influx of "believers" subverted the mandate to evangelize. I felt that Calvary Church needed to break through our evangelical boundaries and touch people who don't go to church anywhere. I even suggested to the church board that we not accept any more members who were believers coming from other churches. (We decided against this.) While I was enjoying teaching the Bible and recognized that the growth was supernaturally impelled, I nevertheless wanted to see more people come to personal faith in Christ.

Getting Started

I decided to discuss my concerns with the board. I asked permission to get a small committee together to explore how we could reach more unchurched people. I talked about the old Youth For Christ rallies in the Grand Rapids area. Many of the board members had attended these rallies as teenagers and had seen God work in miraculous ways. I suggested the idea of a Youth For Christ Rally for the Eighties. I was given permission to explore the idea and report back to the board.

With that approval I called together a small group of people who had expressed a high level of interest in an innovative program or service. These people were not blind loyalists to tradition and, like me, they shared a passion for unchurched people:

Jill: An attorney who was a relatively new believer and who struggled with fitting into traditional churches—including Calvary

Craig
and Lisa: A BMW-driving couple who were in the fast track of Yuppiedom (and have since shifted into Christian ministry)

Phil: A composer and musician who produced a "radical" youth rally in New Jersey in the early seventies

Hugh: The minister of worship and music at Calvary, who sang professionally with a rock group in the seventies

Becky: A professor of communications at a local Roman Catholic college

Karen: An author, composer, and creative playwright who, although she was a lifelong member of traditional churches, never quite fit the mold

At the first meeting the group identified two major questions for ongoing discussion:

1. Who are we trying to reach? (Target audience)
2. What kind of a service is most likely to reach them?

These questions were discussed in many meetings over several months. We identified our target audience as unchurched people between the ages of twenty and forty. We then began listing the characteristics of a service that these people would relate to:

- Informal
- Contemporary (nontraditional)
- No pressure for involvement or commitment
- Relevant to these people's needs
- Casual, "laid-back" format
- Visually appealing

As we fleshed out these traits in some detail, several program elements emerged:

- *Informal:* We decided on a code of informal dress. The ushers, musicians, and I would all wear blue jeans (or other informal garb).
- *Contemporary:* We decided on contemporary music (Christian and non-Christian rock) led by a band composed of a lead guitar, bass guitar, synthesizer, piano, and drums. We chose this musical style for several reasons: (1) it is the primary musical language of our target audience, (2) it is definitely *not* traditional, and (3) it engages the audience through tapping their feet and moving their bodies to the beat.
- *No pressure:* We decided there would be no public invitations or "altar calls." No one would be put on the spot or asked to identify oneself or sign anything. We felt anonymity was important to unchurched people.
- *Relevant:* We decided that the topics we discussed should be relevant to the needs of the people who attend. We felt that using an open question-and-answer format would be sensitive to the people.
- *Casual:* "Casual" was difficult to define. We wanted a program that was not intense or high pressured. A formal person preaching a formal sermon behind a formal pulpit would not do. A hand-held mike and stool seemed more appropriate, along with a low-keyed "talk."
- *Visually appealing:* We decided to engage people by using drama. We would redecorate the platform so it did not look like a church platform. We would use stark colors—black, hot pink, and blue.

We also wrestled with a mission statement. We agreed on the following, which has served us well throughout the development, growth, and evaluation of our seeker-sensitive service. The purpose of "Saturday Night" is

To win the right to be heard by addressing the issues of today in order to reach people in our community for Christ. Through a non-conventional Saturday evening service, we will provide a comfortable atmosphere of love and acceptance for attendees that will encourage them to seek Christ. This service will be a pre-evangelistic outreach and will provide an opportunity to share Christ and to teach the basic truths of Scripture.

Getting Down to the Nitty-Gritty

Identifying our target audience and developing the characteristics of a program that it would relate to was only a small part of the task of beginning the seeker-sensitive service. We decided to arrange the committee's work according to several categories: topics, program development, advertising, personnel commitment, and budget.

1. Topics. Unchurched people tend to think that the church is irrelevant. We knew it was important to deal with topics of interest to them. Several people on the committee were assigned to research this matter and recommend appropriate topics. From their research and recommendations we identified six major issues. We decided to phrase these topics in the form of questions, since part of the program would be devoted to a question-and-answer forum.

Eventually we developed a statement to describe the service: "A place to answer questions." To this day we find that attendance fluctuates with the level of interest in the designated topic. We still spend large amounts of time identifying topics and phrasing them in the form of captivating questions. These were the first six topics used in the services:

- Why Is the Church Full of Hypocrites?
- Would Jesus Be a TV Evangelist?
- Is God a Democrat?
- Is Religion for Wimps?
- Would Jesus Wear a Rolex?
- Sex?

2. Program development. The group assigned to develop the program also dealt with ushering, child care, setup of the stage, sound, and lights.

3. Advertising. Phil was assigned this responsibility. He recommended placing ads in the movie section of the newspaper, radio commercials on "easy-listening" rock stations (*not* Christian stations), and billboard advertising along major highways around the city. He researched the costs of these media.

4. Personnel commitment. We commissioned the persons responsible for a specific part of the program to recruit the people necessary to staff it: music, drama, advertising, ushering, child care, and so on. A person was assigned to oversee each area.

5. Budget. Craig was assigned to develop an overall budget for six weekly services. The figure came in at $15,000.

Making the Presentation to the Board

After almost six months of planning the committee was ready to present the idea for board approval. As I reflect on the process, several key factors in the presentation stand out. These factors also served as guidelines for presenting the concept to the congregation later on.

- Our current traditional services will not reach many unchurched people in our community.
- We do not know if this new seeker service will work, but we want to try it for six weeks on an experimental basis.
- The service is designed for twenty-to-forty-year-olds.
- If you are over forty, the service will offend you—don't come.
- The dress is casual—blue jeans recommended.
- You will not hear this music on Sunday, and you will not hear "Sunday" music on Saturday.
- We will evaluate the program after six weeks and decide whether or not to continue.
- We will reserve judgment on the service until the end of

the six-week period. Do not judge it after attending just one time.

- If you decide to attend, you will probably feel uncomfortable because the service will be radically different from anything else the church does.

I felt we should be entirely *honest* with the board and the congregation. I knew the music would be offensive to older adults, so we said that up front. I encouraged people *not* to attend if they despised contemporary music. (Of course, many did attend to see what the service was like, but they were aware of what they were getting into.)

The church board unanimously approved a six-week series as an experiment, with a budget of $15,000. Several members expressed concern—especially about the music— and feared that opening the door to nontraditional ministry would eventually lead to nontraditional ministry on a Sunday morning. They were concerned about the potential criticism and division with the church.

After receiving approval from the board, I began announcing the new series. I was careful to report that the board had unanimously approved the concept on an experimental basis. I wanted the congregation to know that "Saturday Night" was more than my idea—the entire board was behind it. I kept repeating the nine key factors I have identified. By the time "Saturday Night" began, most of the congregation could recite the nine factors by heart. In fact, many joked that they were over forty and planned to be offended when they attended for the first time.

I accepted Christ when I was fourteen years old. The only thing is, I didn't give him control of my life. I fell into a group of people that were into doing drugs and drinking alcohol, and in order to belong to something, I chose to take that path. God tried to get my attention in many ways. I totaled out three cars and a motorcycle and was drinking each time. But it took a divorce for God to really let me know that he was looking for me.

I was a selfish person. I always did things on my own through my own power, and God was a last resort. When I got divorced I finally decided that there were some things in my life that weren't quite right, and I decided to change those things. So about a year and a half ago I came to church for the first time for myself and not for somebody else. I didn't go for my mother, I didn't go because my wife went, I came for me. "Saturday Night" became a part of that because it took me away from doing drugs or wanting to drink, and it gave me an opportunity to come to a place where I could worship with other people.

Pastor Dobson asked me how long I had been a Christian, and I told him I was age fourteen when I accepted Christ—but it's sort of like picking up a hitchhiker. I let Christ into the car, but he wanted to drive, and I said, "No way." So when the divorce came and he finally got my attention, we stopped the car, and I said, "Okay, you drive. You're in charge." It hasn't been easy because I still get into arguments with him about where he wants to lead me and where he wants me to go, but I'm trusting him—I'm learning to trust him.

My wife and I never did reconcile. She was remarried in October of 1992. I look back at the time that was spent waiting for reconciliation and am thankful for it. I was able to strengthen my relationship with God. These days I'm involved in the Greenhouse class, which is for new believers. I attend Bible Study Fellowship and meet with some people one-on-one. It is in this one-on-one discipleship where I have grown a lot and seen other people grow in their relationship to Christ. It is very important that Christians develop relationships with other Christians where accountability can take place. I thank God for outreaches such as "Saturday Night."   —*Kevin Rubley*

CHAPTER 3

LEARNING BY DOING

I was sitting in the front row at the first "Saturday Night." I was dressed in blue jeans, a Chicago Bears sweatshirt, and running shoes without socks. Jazz music was playing over the sound system. To the left of the platform the band members were taking their places: Steve on lead guitar, Danny on rhythm guitar, Brian on bass guitar, Chuck on the synthesizer, Hugh on the electric keyboard, and Burt on the drums. There were monitors and sound cords all over the place. In front of me was a huge sign that read WELCOME TO SATURDAY NIGHT.

I was nervous. As I looked around, I saw some older people who I knew were already uneasy and perhaps angry about what they saw—and the program had not started yet. I reflected on how far I had come from my days at Bob Jones University and Liberty University. *If my mother could see me now,* I thought, *she'd die. She would think she had failed. After all, she was from a Plymouth Brethren background.* But it was too late now to stop the music. The program started, and for better or worse, a dream had come true.

I am not one to get nervous easily. I have been in a few tight spots over the years, but have kept my nerve. I have appeared on the "Phil Donahue Show," on the network news, and in *Time*. None of those events scared me, but "Saturday Night" did. It took more than a year for me to begin feeling a level of comfort with this style of ministry. The whole program was a radical departure from my roots, education, church background, and previous ministry experience. The music set me on edge. The drama often

31

affronted the tastes of traditional churchgoers. Answering questions extemporaneously was intimidating. Having to speak without being "preachy" and to make announcements without church "jargon" was not easy. Five years later, the fear and intimidation are gone, but I continue the learning curve of ministering in a nontraditional setting.

I am persuaded that very little in my theological training and ministry experience prepared me for this new approach to ministry. I seriously doubt that any college or seminary is really preparing students to communicate the gospel to those who are unchurched. To prepare myself, I began reading as much as I could about American culture. I devoured *Time* magazine, the nightly news, films, and the music trends of popular culture. I read best-selling secular books from Donald Trump's *The Art of the Deal* to Louie Anderson's *Dear Dad: Letters from an Adult Child*. When I spoke on Saturday nights, I tried to avoid all theological language in my talks. When I used theological language, I tried to explain it in easy-to-understand terms.

The Six-Week Test

Most of the board members attended at least one of the six programs. After the fifth week we met to evaluate the program and determine whether or not to continue. The compelling argument in favor of continuing was what God had done in the lives of some of the people who came.

After the fifth program I waited around down front and talked with several people. I noticed that after everyone had left, a man in his late twenties was sitting toward the back all alone. I walked over and sat down, and we began to talk.

"What can I do for you?" I asked.

"I was wondering if God could forgive me," he said.

"Of course he can!" I said. "Why do you ask?"

He said he had grown up in a Christian home and had gone to church every week. Seven years ago he got "fed up" with God, left the church, and moved out of his parents' home. He then invited Satan into his life to be his "lord and savior." For the last seven years he had worshiped Satan. He saw the ads for "Saturday Night" and decided to give it a try. He attended all five nights.

I will never forget the prayer he prayed that night. "Dear God," he said, "please forgive me and come into my life. Satan, get out of my life. I now want to live my life for God."

Today Gary still comes to church on Saturday night—and on Sunday. He has grown in his faith in a significant way. He told me he would *never* have walked back into a traditional church, but he felt safe coming to "Saturday Night." When I told the board about Gary and others who had found the Lord, the vote to continue was enthusiastic and unanimous. Not everyone on the board liked the program. Given the chance, they would very likely have changed the dress code and the music. But they recognized that God had used the program in a unique way. I believe God brought Gary into "Saturday Night," not only to meet his need, but to confirm our desires and direction in reaching people in a nontraditional way.

The First Year

The first year was fun. Everything was new and exciting. The attendance was good. Unfortunately, most of the 400–600 attending were either college students or Christian curiosity seekers who wanted to see the "latest thing" in church ministry. But there were also unchurched people, and some of them made commitments to Christ.

As for that first year, I wonder sometimes if we were just pushing the boundaries for their own sakes or if we pushed the boundaries because they were necessary to reach people. Because a large part of the audience was college students, we did many avant-garde things. We had off-beat dramas, "improv" theatre, and hard-hitting music. Often the talk got squeezed into fifteen minutes or less.

The committee continued to meet through the year to evaluate what we were doing. We made several changes. First, we eliminated all congregational singing. Although the songs were simple, contemporary praise songs, the unchurched who came in increasing numbers were hesitant to sing. They didn't know the songs. We felt that by forcing them to sing we were putting them on the spot.

Second, I switched from a lectern to a bar stool. Just sitting down to talk prevented me from drifting into a "Sunday" style of speaking. I traded the lapel mike for a hand-held microphone for the same reason.

Third, we switched from oral questions to written questions. We discovered that people felt greater freedom to ask questions because writing guaranteed anonymity.

The Second Year

At the end of the first year we took the program outdoors for four weeks. We were able to rent an amphitheater in downtown Grand Rapids for these events. The attendance exceeded 1,300 every week. We used the same format, including the question times. Many of the Calvary Church members came to check out what "Saturday Night" was all about. During those weeks I received much criticism about the music: Too loud. Can't understand the words. Not pleasing to God. And so on.

After the outdoor series, we took six weeks off, and during that time I took a hard look at the music. *Maybe those people are right,* I thought. I talked it over with the committee, and we decided to begin the new season with a different style of music. We added about a half-dozen brass players. Although the style was contemporary, it was much different from the pure rock-and-roll style. I thought the change would be good, I was completely wrong.

First, the people who had complained about the music did not see that the new style was any different. Second, over the first few months our attendance fell by about three hundred—mostly college students. Unfortunately, I was too stubborn to change, and we never completely reclaimed the people we lost. Almost every Saturday night someone would write a question complaining about the new musical format. People wanted the old band and the old style back.

The matter of musical style still puzzles me. Our surveys indicate that the most important ingredient of the program is the talk. Music ranks second; only 25 percent think it is the most important element, and 8 percent consider it the least important. Nevertheless, when we changed the music, people stopped coming. It appears that although music is not the primary reason that people come, it is a vital ingredient in their continuing to attend. After three months, we went back to the old band and have not tampered with the music again.

Shortly before we changed to the brass band I was talking with a friend of mine who is associated with a group of fundamentalist churches. I explained my prediction that the style of music was not all that significant and said we were toning the music down. Needless to say, he was delighted. He asked me to write an article for the church group's magazine on how we were moving away from Christian rock. I have not written the article. How could I? I was proved wrong, and we went back to rock.

The Crossroads

By the end of the third year I was discouraged with the progress of "Saturday Night." Our attendance was about three hundred fifty—down more than a hundred from a year earlier. It seemed that we were doing all we could to get it to grow, but "Saturday Night" was going in the opposite direction. Yet the Sunday morning services at Calvary were growing to the point where we were almost out of space.

We discussed the decline of attendance on Saturday night and the space problem of Sunday morning at our summer staff retreat. We decided to recommend that the board drop "Saturday Night" as it currently existed. We suggested replacing it with a duplicate of our Sunday morning service. We would recruit more choir and orchestra. I might even take questions from the audience. But we would have basically the same service as on Sunday morning.

In retrospect, I am not sure how we reached that decision. We felt that a more traditional service would grow faster and take some pressure off Sunday mornings. We felt I could be sensitive and adapt the sermon to an audience with more unchurched people. We knew we might lose some people, but would gain more. The change would be less demanding on the staff in that it would not require a totally different set-up and program.

When I presented the recommendation to the board, they were more than a little surprised. They agreed to support and approve this change, but they were generally uneasy about altering what we had done for three years. I announced publicly what we were going to do. Hugh, the minister of music, had already begun to recruit new people for the choir and orchestra; he was enthusiastic about having a more traditional service.

I took a vacation the week after the board meeting. I began to rethink the decision we had just made. The more I thought, the more I realized that if we changed, we would be back in the traditional trap. We would attract more and more Christians on Saturday night and would lose the hundreds of seekers who had attended "Saturday Night" from time to time. Even though only 300 came in any given week, there were probably more than 1000 unchurched people who attended from time to time. Being unchurched, they didn't show up every week. But when they did, they deserved the kind of program they experienced the last time they had come. By the end of my vacation I was absolutely convinced that dropping the Saturday night seeker service would be a fatal mistake for our evangelistic ministry.

Back in the office, I met with Phil, the "Saturday Night" coordinator. During my absence he had been thinking the same way. We agreed that our recommendation was wrong, and I agreed to go back to the board. I told the board we had made a hasty mistake and asked permission to continue what we had been doing. The board kindly forgave me, and we proceeded into the fourth year.

I learned some important lessons from that experience. First, the growth on "Saturday Night" should not be compared with Sunday attendance. Second, the growth on "Saturday Night" will be slow. Third, at times the attendance may decrease. Fourth, a seeker-sensitive service is a long-term commitment—you cannot just have it for a little while and then go on to something else. Fifth, a seeker-sensitive service is a draining experience that absorbs energy and strength continually. Sixth, until a person makes a commitment to Christ, he or she is not likely to attend on a regular basis.

From a Program to a Church

The fifth year marked a significant change in the "Saturday Night" program. Not only did the attendance significantly increase, but there was also a greater feeling of community and belonging among those who attended. We began to see more and more people returning every week. We have become a separate church within the walls of Calvary Church. Several factors have contributed to this:

1. Options after the programs. We started to offer several sessions after "Saturday Night." One is for singles, and it is usually a discussion about a pertinent topic. The average attendance exceeds one hundred. The second option is a small-group Bible study, which about twenty people attend. Many personal contacts are made in these groups that ultimately lead to a personal commitment to Christ. We have recently added Narcotics Anonymous and Alcoholics Anonymous groups.

2. The Ditch Diggers. The ditch diggers are a group of about fifty people whom we recruited out of the Sunday services. They have received extensive training in personal growth, evangelism, discipleship, and servanthood. They serve on various teams and rotate in the responsibilities of "Saturday Night": ushering, child care, evangelism, follow-up, the set-up and tearing down of the stage. These people became a core for sharing the "Saturday Night" ministry. This has enlarged the ownership of "Saturday Night" beyond a small group of staff and laypeople.

3. Prayer support. We recruited more than three hundred people who pray for "Saturday Night" every day. Few of these people ever attend. I write prayer-letter updates from time to time. I believe that these people have been the key to the remarkable spiritual and numerical growth we experienced in the fifth year.

4. *Wednesday Night.* When we encouraged new believers from "Saturday Night" to try the Sunday services, the results were discouraging. Most of them were overwhelmed. Few of them continued to attend on Sunday. Yet we felt these new believers needed Bible training, so we started a special Wednesday night service. I preach the same sermon that I give on Sunday night, but it is a much less formal service than Sunday night. We also have Awana (a youth program) and other programs on Wednesday night. We now encourage those who want to take the next step beyond "Saturday Night" to try the midweek service. While the jury is still out as to its effectiveness, it appears that people are making that commitment on Wednesdays and not getting lost in the shuffle.

5. *Bible studies.* We offer two Sunday night Bible studies for people who want to explore further what it means to be a Christian. At the first one, more than thirty people attended and more than half of them were nonbelievers. The studies are held in homes—and yes, they are held during our regular Sunday night service. When the six-week study is completed, the people have an opportunity to continue in a new six-week study, and most of them do. And so it goes.

6. *Opportunities for help.* On the back of the program that we regularly hand out at "Saturday Night" are three tear-out cards. One is for writing out questions. The other two are for obtaining help: one about meeting a friend, and the other for talking to someone. The ditch diggers use these cards for personal follow-up.

My parents had been attending Sundays at Calvary for about four years until they talked me into trying "Saturday Night." Now I'm thankful I went.

"Saturday Night" has opened many new doors for me. I was introduced to Bible studies, testimonials of people like me, singles groups. The list goes on and on. "Saturday Night" has brought me a new and truthful understanding of God and his Son. It has also given me options to be able to expand my fellowship with other Christians.

"Saturday Night" is what God knew I need to start learning more about him and his Word. The more I grow to love God, his Son, and the Word, the more of a loving Christian I have and will become. —*Anonymous*

CHAPTER 4

THE BASIC INGREDIENTS OF "SATURDAY NIGHT"

W e have experimented and changed the format of "Saturday Night" several times over its first five years. Each year we survey those who attend about the program. We have settled into a format that seems to work best for us and seems to relate well to the target audience. While we are open to learn and change, we have remained pretty consistent with this format for the last two years.

Music

The two aspects of church ministry that bring the most intense disagreement among church people are the level of the thermostat and the style of music. You will *never* please everyone on either of these issues. Even though the people of Calvary Church are tolerant of the musical style on "Saturday Night," many do not like it and wish we would change. The most frequent complaints:

- It's too loud.
- I can't understand the words.
- It's wild.
- Why can't you just sing hymns?
- It's of Satan.
- God is grieved.

In deciding on the style of music for "Saturday Night," we considered a number of factors.

1. The reason for rock. I have deliberately chosen the word *rock* to describe the predominant style of the "Saturday Night" music. I have avoided the word *contemporary* as being too broad. I know of a Christian university that banned its students from a Steve Green concert because he is a "contemporary" artist. Others consider Sandi Patti contemporary. The style of "Saturday Night" is basically late sixties and early seventies rock. We have a lead guitar, a bass guitar, a synthesizer, a piano, drums, and sometimes a saxophone.

Some weeks the music is "hot." Other weeks it is more jazz or folk—once in a while with a little country. The band plays three songs in the program, including one during the offering, and they usually relate to the topic of the evening. Sometimes we will have secular songs if they relate to the topic:

- "Give Me Something to Believe In" by Poison
- "Imagine" by John Lennon
- "Coming Out of the Dark" by Gloria Estefan

Why did we choose this style? First, we live in Grand Rapids, Michigan, a city with 480 Protestant churches. It is bound by several religious traditions, and many unchurched people are turned off by all the traditions. We wanted people who attend "Saturday Night" to know immediately that it is not a traditional service. We felt that one way to achieve this is through the musical style we choose. Not more than a handful of churches in Grand Rapids open with a live band every week. We wanted to be radical because it was necessary to break the mold of expectation in a conservative community.

Second, we wanted a style of music that communicated to people aged twenty to forty-five. That style of music, without question, is rock. It is the language of my generation. It is the musical style that I love and listen to. It communicates in a language that I understand.

Third, we wanted a musical style that would elicit a response. Unchurched people come to a service hesitantly. Their mind-set is "you're not going to get me." Their defenses are up. We felt that a style of music that would get them moving in a physical way (nodding heads and tapping feet) would help break down their defenses. This does not mean that the crowd are on their feet banging heads and clapping; they seldom clap during a song, but they always applaud at the end.

2. *There is a time and place for everything.* If the "Saturday Night" band were to play at the traditional service on Sunday morning, there would be war immediately. Some people attempt to change the style of music in a traditional service to accommodate Christian rock, but I think that this is a mistake. If you make people angry with what you do, how can you lead them in worship? We learned this lesson the hard way.

After several years of "Saturday Night," Hugh, the minister of worship, had a "gospel" jazz band perform at a Sunday night service. The band played for the congregational singing, did the offertory and accompanied a singles singing group. It took weeks to recover. People were angry. The people who tolerated "hot" music on "Saturday Night" were not willing to tolerate it on Sunday. I learned that it is imperative to keep seeker-sensitive services and traditional services separate. They do *not* mix. And if you mingle the musical styles, you are very likely to harm both services.

3. *Expect opposition.* Our first night outdoors in downtown Grand Rapids with the "Saturday Night" service was exciting. On one side of the amphitheater was a group of "punk" teenagers who stayed through the entire program. After the first song, there was a disturbance at the back of the crowd. Several young men were waving protest placards proclaiming that the music was of Satan. They continued to interrupt the program until they were arrested by the police. I found it incredible that as we were trying to share the gospel with people who would never attend church even for "Saturday Night," several "Christians" were protesting against us.

Anyone using rock music in church services should expect to receive opposition and criticism. It may not be as glaring as protesters with signs, but it will be there. I have tried to respond to this criticism in a sensitive way without arguing with people. The following chart lists my responses to the objections I hear most frequently:

Rock Music: Why?

Objection	Response
You should not use contemporary music.	All Christian music was contemporary at one time. If the church had always rejected contemporary music, we would not have the hymns of Charles Wesley, Ira D. Sankey, Fanny J. Crosby, or John W. Peterson.
Rock music is secular music.	Music is neither secular nor sacred, neither good nor bad in itself. What is important is how we use it and what it says.
It is too loud.	It may be too loud for you, but it is not too loud for people who like it.
I don't like it.	That's okay. That style is not for you. If it makes you angry, don't attend "Saturday Night."
I don't understand the words.	Fine! I do, and so do the people who attend "Saturday Night." Rock is a language and style they understand.
Rock music is not biblical.	There is no such a thing as a "biblical" style of music. The book of Psalms is a book of musical selections; the words were preserved without error until today, but we do not know the musical score or the style used with them. If God had intended a biblical style of music, he certainly could have revealed more about it in the Bible.
Rock music is associated with sex,	You are right that most of the secular rock music is rotten; I often

drugs, and rebellion. It has no place in the church.

speak against it. But that does not mean the style itself is rotten. Men who wear their hair short and dress in gray suits with button-down shirt collars are businessmen. Yet that "uniform" is associated with greed and materialism. But we do not condemn conservative suits. Nor should we condemn a musical style because it is associated with some ungodly people.

I am concerned about where this will lead us down the road. If we tolerate rock music now, what will be next?

I am also concerned about the future, but my concern is to pass the truth to the next generation—not our preferences and traditions. If we do what is right today, God will take care of tomorrow.

I am often asked, "Couldn't you do 'Saturday Night' without that style of music?" I usually answer, "We probably could, but it would not be as effective. In fact, we did back off for several months and ended up losing several hundred people who attended."

Drama

The second major ingredient in the Saturday Night service is drama. The drama always relates to the topic for the evening, and it has become a powerful support for the talk. I usually refer to the drama by way of illustration in my talk. Over the years we have experimented with various approaches to drama. For the first two years we had at least two sketches each night, one related to the topic and the other unrelated. We did monologues, pantomime, and improvisational theatre. In our evaluation we concluded that drama unconnected to the topic was superfluous. It was entertaining, but our focus is not primarily entertainment.

Some people question the validity of drama in the context

of any church service. Eugene H. Peterson raises this issue in his book *Working the Angles*.

> Hebrews and Christians, aware of the enormous difference between themselves and the Greeks, and the critical necessity of preserving their *word*-ness over against the Greek *image*-ness, kept their distance from nude bodies and theaters. From our perspective that looks like prudery, and maybe it did decline into that, but at root it was protection against the danger of the powerful visual stimuli of statuary and drama seducing them into a religion of aestheticism, away from the moral/spiritual intensities of faith. They knew how easy it was for the ardor of obedient listening to be diluted into amused watching, and took measures to guard their aural concentration. They sensed that surrounding themselves with all those god-images reduced them to less than they knew themselves to be. Religion as entertainment is always more attractive, but it is also less true. It is pretty poor stuff compared to the word. Paul sarcastically asked the Galatians if they preferred "the weak and beggarly elemental spirits, whose slaves you want to be once more?" (Gal. 4:9).[1]

I see inherent dangers in a "visually" oriented approach to church in contrast with a "listening" approach. But that does not mean visual stimuli are wrong per se. If something visual replaces the spoken, listened-to word, then it is very likely pure entertainment. But if it supports the spoken word, it becomes another way to illustrate truth. Just as the Old Testament prophets often illustrated truth with their actions and just as Jesus often illustrated truth with parables, so also can drama be a highly effective way of illustrating truth. In fact, I could probably recollect most of the drama sketches we have done in "Saturday Night," but would have a hard time recalling the content of my talks on those nights.

"Real Life"

"Real Life" is an element of the program we added in about the fourth year. It is basically a personal testimony.

[1]*Working the Angles* (Grand Rapids: Eerdmans, 1987).

The speaker may be someone who has struggled with the issue at hand that night. The testimony always concerns what Christ has done in that person's life. The speaker goes to the platform without introduction and begins, "My name is _____, and I would like to tell you what Christ has done in my life." The speakers are usually nervous, and some read from cards. Sometimes I interview the people. But it is obvious to the crowd that these are real people talking about real life with real solutions from God. I encourage the speakers to be honest. Most of them express both the excitement of their relationship with Christ and their ongoing struggles.

Announcements and Offering

The tendency in traditional churches is to handle the announcements and offering extemporaneously as not being all that critical to the service overall. At "Saturday Night" I word announcements very carefully. I follow the same format each week:

1. I welcome the crowd.
2. I announce the topic for the evening and the topic for next week.
3. I explain the question-answer format and how the audience can ask questions.
4. I announce what sessions are held after the program and offer opportunities that might interest the crowd.
5. I talk about the offering.

Yes, we pass a plate and collect an offering. Of all the elements of the service, the offering receives the most opposition from believers who attend "Saturday Night." They feel a collection is offensive to nonbelievers. We have discussed this issue many times, but we concluded that at some point, anyone associated with Calvary Church will experience a plate's being passed. We decided to get over that hurdle sooner than later. I carefully introduce the offering this way: "If you are visiting tonight, please do not put anything in the offering. The offering is for those who regularly attend and want to give. All the money goes to underwriting the expenses of 'Saturday Night.' So please do not feel any pressure to put money in the plate. We are glad you came, and we hope you enjoy the rest of the program."

Scripture Reading

Reading from the Bible is another element we added in midcourse. Before I speak, someone reads a Scripture passage related to the topic; it is often the main passage that I refer to in my talk. Reading the Scripture reinforces our commitment to be biblical in what we do Saturday night. After reading the Scripture, the person leads in prayer.

The Talk

I usually speak at least twenty-five minutes and allow ten to fifteen minutes for questions afterward. This means that more than half the service is devoted to verbal teaching. All our surveys indicate that the talk and the "Q and A" are the main reason that people attend "Saturday Night." There are two important aspects of this part of the service.

1. The content of the talk. John R. Stott offers an excellent model of preaching in his book *Between Two Worlds.* He states that preaching begins in the world of biblical truth and builds a bridge into the world of everyday living. This is the approach I use at Sunday Services: I usually teach from the Bible verse by verse, then I try to apply the truth in practical ways to my life and the lives of the congregation. However, I do *not* use that model at "Saturday Night." Instead, I do the reverse: I begin in the real world of everyday life, and I stay in that world for most of the talk. Eventually I turn to the world of biblical truth to demonstrate that the Bible is relevant for today.

This approach is much more difficult and time-consuming to prepare than what I do on Sunday. It requires much reading in nonbiblical sources. I now buy more nontheological, nonbiblical books than traditional "pastor's" books. I read best-sellers. I consume *Time* magazine. I see some of the latest movies. I try to integrate all these things into my talks.

One time I introduced a talk about God by identifying some of the strange concepts people have about him:

1. *Terminator III*. Some people think that God is nothing more than the great destroyer in the sky. He is sitting up there waiting for us to mess up so he can blow us away.
2. *Peter Pan*. Some people think God is this nice person in tight, green pants who goes around in a magical kingdom fighting Captain Hook.
3. *George Burns* (As in *Oh, God!*). Some people think God is an old, kind, funny grandfather with a cigar in his mouth.

People relate to these movies and, it is hoped, gain insight into their own concepts of God.

In a series on forgiveness I referred frequently to Suzanne Sommer's book *Keeping Secrets* and Anderson's *Dear Dad*. These are powerful books about dealing with parental abuse.

Dear Dad,

Why don't I know you better? I figure you spent several hours a day for 40 years drinking. Multiply that by 365 days, then divide by 60 minutes and then divide again by 24 hours. That's more than a 1,000 days you spent with alcohol. In other words, that's more than three years you spent with alcohol instead of your family.

I was alive for twenty-seven of those years, and I missed you.

Louie Anderson[2]

In the book Louie works through the process of forgiving his father.

[2]*Dear Dad: Letters from an Adult Child* (New York: Viking-Penguin, 1991), p. 103.

This last picture is a close-up of you. There is a cigarette in your mouth, and you're wearing the same hat and glasses that I have on now. I see the look on your face, in your eyes, and you're looking directly at me, and I hear you say, "I love you, Louie."

I know, Dad.

I forgive you. I understand.

I realize why I have come here and what I've been looking for all this time. I wanted to be with you. And now I am and always will be.

Oh yeah. There's one more thing that I haven't said but want to. And that one thing is, I love you.

Your son,
Louie[3]

Reading excerpts from these letters opened a door to what the Bible says and how to forgive those who hurt you.

2. *The delivery of the talk.* I have worked hard at delivering the talk without preaching. First, I dress in casual clothes such as blue jeans and a T-shirt to invite a relaxed, informal atmosphere. Second, I sit on a bar stool and use a hand-held microphone. When I walk around as I talk, I tend to get "preachy." Sitting down, I tend to be more conversational in style.

Questions and Answers

The most intimidating part of "Saturday Night" is the Q and A. I have no advance knowledge of the questions, and no one sorts through them before I read them. The back of the program has a tear-off section for written questions. The ushers collect these questions after the talk, and when I read them aloud it is the first time I hear the question.

The Q and A is a distinctive feature of "Saturday Night," and several times a year we devote the entire talk time to an open forum. People respond very well. It also enables the planners to know the kinds of problems people are facing. We keep all the questions on file and use them as a basis for planning future topics.

[3]Ibid., pp. 208–9.

Prayer

At the end of the program I ask everyone to stand for a closing prayer. This is usually the second time we pray at "Saturday Night." (For the first three years we did not pray at all.) In the prayer I mention the people who asked personal questions, and I summarize a main thought from the talk.

What We Do Not Do

In the first few years we had some congregational singing. (After all, Willow Creek uses congregational singing, so we thought we should too.) But few people sang. We concluded that the unchurched people who attended did not want to sing, so why force them to do it? We dropped the congregational singing and are glad that we did.

Even though I was raised in a Christian home, I never thought much about people without Christ. Not until after our first child died and I saw the brevity of life did I realize the importance of reaching people with the good news of the gospel. I was challenged to give my life for the only two things that are eternal: God's Word and people.

The "Saturday Night" service has been and continues to be a wonderful opportunity for me personally to be involved in this goal of giving my life for things that will last forever. My husband and I stay after the service to be available to talk with and listen to people who are searching and hurting. What overwhelms me is the many, many people that come through those doors every Saturday night with incredible pain in their lives! It is a great privilege for me to see firsthand and talk with so many who haven't walked into a church in years but do come to "Saturday Night." Many of these people are desparately searching for truth and meaning to their lives. They have tried to find answers in other places, things, and relationships, but nothing fills that void.

I am challenged by Matthew 9:9–12, when Jesus called Matthew to be his disciple. Jesus had dinner at his house with many tax collectors and sinners. The Pharisees criticized him, but Jesus so eloquently answered, "It is not the healthy who need a doctor, but the sick. But go and learn what this means; I desire mercy, not sacrifice. For I have not come to call the righteous but sinners." This to me sums up our "Saturday Night": a place where people can come as they are, to be loved, accepted. and have their questions answered. I consider it a great joy and privilege to be a part of it.   —*Mary Zuidema*

CHAPTER 5

THE BIBLICAL BASIS
FOR SEEKER MINISTRY

Though I am free and belong to no man, I make myself a slave to everyone, to win as many as possible. To the Jews I became like a Jew, to win the Jews. To those under the law I became like one under the law (though I myself am not under the law), so as to win those under the law. To those not having the law I became like one not having the law (though I am not free from God's law but am under Christ's law), so as to win those not having the law. To the weak I became weak, to win the weak. I have become all things to all men so that by all possible means I might save some. I do all this for the sake of the gospel, that I may share in its blessings.

Do you not know that in a race all the runners run, but only one gets the prize? Run in such a way as to get the prize. Everyone who competes in the games goes into strict training. They do it to get a crown that will not last; but we do it to get a crown that will last forever. Therefore I do not run like a man running aimlessly; I do not fight like a man beating the air. No, I beat my body and make it my slave so that after I have preached to others, I myself will not be disqualified for the prize (1 Cor. 9:19–27, NIV).

*M*uch of the criticism directed toward seeker-sensitive services describes them as "market-driven," "pragmatically directed," and "consumer-oriented." The underlying assumption is that the whole idea lacks a biblical foundation or, worse, that this approach to ministry violates the Bible.

I confess that when we started our service, we were not operating under some new understanding of biblical principles. We began "Saturday Night" to reach unchurched people without identifying a biblical basis for our methods. But as the service grew, we were challenged by others to defend our actions from Scripture. So we were forced to examine our strategies according to biblical principles.

"A MAP"

The primary theme of the apostle Paul's statement in 1 Corinthians 9 is "to win as many as possible."

Notice the last four words of this phrase. The first letters of each word form the acronym A M A P—"a map." Paul is giving the church and believers a map—a guide—for reaching their destination. The destination is winning as many as possible to Christ.

As I have stated, the most important prerequisite for starting a seeker-sensitive service is a passion for evangelism. If evangelism is not the map you are following, do not venture into a seeker-sensitive service. Paul had that passion: "I have become all things to all men so that by all possible means I might save some."

"A MAP" Demands Flexibility, Adjustment, and Change

There is no single, exclusive way to do evangelism biblically. Paul identifies at least three different strategies. These strategies center in three separate people groups: the Jews, the Gentiles, and the weak.

1. Reaching the Jews

To the Jews I became like a Jew, to win the Jews. To those under the law [namely Jews] I became like one under the law (though I myself am not under the law), so as to win those under the law (vv. 20–21).

When evangelizing the Jews, Paul adapted his strategy to the cultural practices of the Jews. He ate Jewish food; he spoke the language of the Jews; he followed Jewish tradition. This strategy is played out repeatedly during Paul's missionary journeys.

From Perga they went on to Pisidian Antioch. On the Sabbath they entered the synagogue and sat down. . . . "The God of the people of Israel chose our fathers; he made the people prosper during their stay in Egypt, with mighty power he led them out of that country" (Acts 13:14, 17).

On the next Sabbath almost the whole city gathered to hear the word of the Lord. . . . Then Paul and Barnabas answered them boldly: "We had to speak the word of God to you first. Since you reject it and do not consider yourselves worthy of eternal life, we now turn to the Gentiles" (Acts 13:44, 46).

In this context, Paul was evangelizing the Jews and those who accepted and believed the Old Testament Scriptures. He quoted the Old Testament and reviewed Jewish history. This is biblically based evangelism; it is a case study in exegetically based evangelism. If this were the only example of evangelism in Paul's ministry, we could safely conclude that *all* evangelism must follow this method: You must review the Bible, quote the Bible, explain the Bible. To do less is to violate the Bible. And there are people who preach and teach that. But that is *not* the only case study. The second identifiable people group in 1 Corinthians 9 is the Gentiles.

2. The Gentiles

To those not having the law [the Gentiles] I became like one not having the law (though I am not free from God's law, but am under Christ's law), so as to win those not having the law (v. 21).

The Jews were not the only group who needed the gospel; the Gentiles needed it as well. But Paul had a different strategy for the Gentiles. When he was with the Jews he acted like a Jew, but when he was with the Gentiles he acted like a Gentile. He talked like a Gentile and ate with the Gentiles. In other words, Paul behaved with the Gentiles in ways he would never do with the Jews and vice versa. Paul not only taught this flexibility, but also lived it.

"For as I walked around and looked carefully at your objects of worship, I even found an altar with this inscription: TO AN UNKNOWN GOD. Now what you worship as something unknown I am going to proclaim to you. The God who made the world and everything in it is the Lord of heaven and earth and does not live in temples built by hands. . . . 'For in him we live and move and have our being.' As some of your own poets have said, 'We are his offspring'" (Acts 17:23–24, 28).

In this passage Paul shared the gospel with Gentiles who were *not* familiar with the Old Testament or the God of the Jews. On Mars Hill he was surrounded by the images of the various gods whom these Gentiles worshiped. The Gentiles had erected an altar entitled "To an Unknown God" to ensure that they did not overlook any deities. Paul began with that altar and declared that he would tell them the name of the "Unknown God."

We might think that at this point Paul would begin quoting the Bible. Wrong! Paul did not quote one verse from the Old Testament, review an Old Testament story, or even use the Hebrew name for God. Rather, he spoke in the language of pagan philosophers and his only quotation was from pagan poets. Yet he concluded on the same theme as in the synagogue—the resurrection of Jesus Christ. But he chose a completely different route to get there. Different people, different culture, different strategy—same gospel.

3. The Weak

To the weak I became weak, to win the weak. I have become all things to all men so that by all possible means I might save some (1 Cor. 9:22).

The third identifiable people group in this passage is the weak. First Corinthians 10 explains who these people are.

If some unbeliever invites you to a meal and you want to go, eat whatever is put before you without raising questions of conscience. But if anyone says to you, "This has been offered in sacrifice," then do not eat it, both for the sake of the man who told you and for conscience' sake—the other man's conscience, I mean, not yours. For why should my freedom be judged by another's conscience? (vv. 27–29).

In many Gentile cities in the ancient world people offered animal sacrifices to pagan gods. Some of the best meat was saved from these animals, and the priests sold it in the market to assist the temple treasury. This meat was a source of controversy. Some people—including believers and nonbelievers—bought and ate the meat. Others among them refused to eat this meat because it was associated with the temple and pagan worship. Now, the governing principle of Scripture is that meat is meat. There is nothing inherently immoral about any kind of meat, including meat offered to gods. However, some people were still bothered by eating it and were referred to as having a "weak" conscience.

In 1 Corinthians 10, Paul dealt with the situation of a believer who dines in the home of a nonbeliever. Paul said not to ask questions about the food the host sets before you. But if someone says that it is meat offered to idols, then do not eat it. The implication is that the person who raises the issue of the meat is a nonbeliever who is bothered by eating this kind of meat. Paul said that to respect the other person's conscience you, too, should decline; otherwise you may hinder your ability to talk about Christ.

Three groups and three strategies. "To win as many as possible" demands flexibility, adjustment, and change. Paul adapted his strategy according to the people group he was reaching. In the language of missiology we call it "cross-cultural identification." Paul said, "I have become all this to all men so that by all possible means I may save some. I do all this for the sake of the gospel, that I may share in its blessings" (1 Cor. 9:22–23).

Let me issue a warning. This kind of zeal for evangelism can get us in trouble because what we do in different places to reach different people will often seem contradictory. Such was the case with Paul.

Day 1:   Lunch with nonbelieving Jews. Paul eats a kosher meal and spends his time discussing and debating the Old Testament Scriptures. He is careful in his behavior and actions. He follows *all* the details of Jewish law and tradition.

Day 2: Lunch with nonbelieving Gentiles. Paul eats a ham sandwich and enjoys some meat offered to idols. He does not even mention the Bible, but instead discusses philosophy and poetry.

Day 3: Lunch with the weak. Paul eats gentile food, but he declines meat offered to idols because it could hinder his freedom to share the gospel.

Observe the contradictions of those three days. This is the way Paul lived. He understood that different circumstances demanded different behaviors, but that all circumstances demanded the gospel. Paul understood that it was *not* wrong to eat kosher food with the Jews, nor was it wrong to eat nonkosher food with the Gentiles. He understood it was *not* wrong to quote from poetry and not the Bible with the Gentiles. He understood it was not wrong to eat meat offered to idols one day and not the next.

Our problem today is that we place these different methods in the context of right and wrong. We say that the only right way to do evangelism is to quote the Bible or that the only right music that communicates the gospel is traditional music. We say that our style of worship, preaching, and teaching is the only right way and that the unchurched must meet us on our terms.

Paul refused to moralize methods and chose to meet nonbelievers on their turf. He was willing to abandon religious tradition and legalistic expectations when doing so advanced the gospel. Our problem is that when we defend and protect religious traditions for their own sake, we fail miserably in getting out the gospel.

I accompanied forty senior high students on a ministry trip to Barcelona, Spain. They did street ministry that included music, drama, puppets, and gymnastics. What they did on the streets of Spain could not take place on the platform of our church on Sunday morning. For example, some of the background music for gymnastics is completely secular.

The gymnastics team was performing on a plaza in downtown Barcelona, and the music from the movie *Rocky* began to play. Ten blocks away, an American from New York City heard the music. This young man felt lost in the Spanish culture but was learning the language. Then he heard this "wonderful" American music and walked ten blocks to find out what was going on. He happened to sit next to me. I handed him a tract and began talking in Spanish. He said, "I speak English." I said, "Great, so do I." He was a Christian, but for two years he had walked away from God, the church, and the Scriptures. But before we left the plaza, he recommitted his life to Jesus Christ. He was in church the next day. Because we sang hymns? No. Because floating between the buildings ten blocks away was the theme from *Rocky*.

Our group was in another plaza several days later, a plaza surrounded by apartment buildings. More than a thousand people were watching the program. We began the gymnastics. Up on the eighth or ninth floor was a college student who heard the theme from *Rocky* and wondered, *What in the world is going on*? He looked down. All our gymnasts were wearing purple, baggy "Hammer" pants and white shirts and were jumping over a vault. The student said to his mother, "It looks like angels down there going over a vault and flipping in the air. God must want to say something to us and I'm going down to hear what he has to say." Because we were singing hymns? No. Floating through a building was the theme from *Rocky*. I know Sylvester Stallone had no idea when he created the movie—in which he speaks only one intelligible sentence—that the music could be used on the streets of Barcelona to attract some people to hear a message from God.

Why do we have "Saturday Night"? Because if we are going to reach people for Jesus Christ, we have to take all possible means, in all possible ways, to reach some people. At times that will seem inconsistent. In our setting on

Sunday, we do things a certain way. On "Saturday Night" we do them a certain way. On the streets of Spain we do them a certain way. In the high school department we do them a certain way.

We may appear to be contradicting ourselves, but we are not. We may appear to be inconsistent, but we are not. We recognize that there is no single, exclusive *right* way to share Jesus Christ. To win as many as possible demands flexibility, adjustment, and change.

"A MAP" Demands Restraint

Do you not know that in a race all the runners run, but only one gets the prize? Run in such a way as to get the prize. Everyone who competes in the games goes into strict training. They do it to get a crown that will not last; but we do it to get a crown that will last forever. Therefore I do not run like a man running aimlessly; I do not fight like a man beating the air. No, I beat my body and make it my slave so that after I have preached to others, I myself will not be disqualified for the prize (1 Cor. 9:24–27).

We might assume from Paul's principle "by all possible means" that winning people to Christ allows absolute freedom from restraint. Wrong! Paul balances his practice of flexibility with the demand of restraint. He speaks of the restraint of "strict training" and making his body his "slave."

1. *The Restraint of Strict Training.* The July 1992 issue of *Runner's World* magazine had an article called "Run to Win."

You'll probably never win an Olympic gold medal, but the methods that work for the Olympic greats will also improve your training and racing (p. 82).

The article listed ten things important to improving one's running, based on interviews with runners who have won Olympic medals.

How do you get to the victory stand? The same way you get to Carnegie Hall: practice, man practice. To be the best in the world requires years of hard training. Day-in, day-out training. Training that gets progressively harder as your body adapts to it: faster repetitions with shorter recovery intervals; special workouts to overcome weaknesses; heavier weights when you're lifting. You need to push to your limits and beyond (p. 82).

Joan Benoit Samuelson remembers feeling such mental toughness as she stood at the starting line of the first women's Olympic marathon in 1984: "I was sure nobody had worked as hard as I had. I was fit, I was healthy, I was confident" (p. 83). And she won the gold medal. She added, "Everything else gets pushed to the side. Your event becomes the top priority, and you schedule everything around it" (p. 83). Running—or any endeavor at the elite level—demands sacrifice.

Frank Shorter, another medalist in the Olympic marathon, recalls, "Everything I did from 1969 to 1972 was in terms of, how will this get me to the Olympic Games? It affects what you eat, how you train, how you race—everything you do" (p. 83).

The apostle Paul expressed the same attitude in 1 Corinthians 9. Everything he did was in terms of how it would help him to win more people to Jesus Christ. Can we say that as a church? Are we willing to do whatever it takes for successful evangelism?

The restraint of strict training demands that we set aside everything that would hinder us in sharing the gospel and focus on one objective only—to win as many as possible. This same idea is articulated in the letter to the Hebrews.

Therefore, since we are surrounded by such a great cloud of witnesses, let us throw off everything that hinders and the sin that so easily entangles, and let us run with perseverance the race marked out for us. Let us fix our eyes on Jesus, the author and perfecter of our faith, who for the joy set before him endured the cross, scorning its shame, and sat down at the right hand of the throne of God (Heb. 12:1–2).

Two areas of restraint are identified by the writer. First, we must get rid of everything that hinders. Second, we must eliminate sin. Getting rid of everything that hinders means eliminating inappropriate things even if they are good, moral, and right. In other words, Paul said, "If you are going to run the hundred-meter sprint, don't wear a suit, carry a backpack, or bring your portable lap computer." All these things have their place, but in a race they will merely hold you back.

This is true in the ministry of a church. When we face new programs, new ideas, and new opportunities, we ought to ask one question: "Will this enable us to win as many as possible to Jesus Christ?" I am often asked, "Why don't you start a Christian day school at Calvary Church?" Christian education has a role, but I have no heart's desire or commitment to have our church start a school. A school is good and in certain contexts necessary, but I do not see it fitting the mandate to win as many as possible to Jesus Christ. Others have a burden and a vision for that. But the consuming objective at Calvary Church is evangelism, and we do not want to expend energy in any program that does not advance our objective. If we bought into every program, every idea, and every concept that other people do, we would dilute the vision. Our map must always be "Will this help us win as many as possible to Jesus Christ?" Like Frank Shorter, we need to decide that every focus, every choice, and every decision will serve our purpose.

The second thing we must eliminate is sin. "The sin that so easily entangles us" hinders evangelism. Unconfessed sin inhibits us from making progress in the race God has called us to run. Professing one thing and living another is a great obstacle to sharing the good news of Jesus Christ. Have you ever heard someone say, "All of this is good, but I work with this guy or I work with this woman and he/she claims to be a Christian and they do A-B-C and D. If that's Christianity . . ."? Believers who embrace sin and get entangled in sin wreak damaging consequences for the cause of the gospel. Sin distracts and weighs us down. It inhibits the race.

2. The Discipline of Keeping Your Body Under Subjection. Personal purity is an absolute prerequisite for effective evangelism. Unchurched people can see through hypocrisy, legalism, inconsistency, and impurity. Even though they may be guilty of the same things, they expect a level of integrity in people who claim to know Christ. They do not expect perfection, but they do expect believers to be honestly seeking to live for God.

Sometime after we began "Saturday Night," Calvary Church voted to expand its facilities to provide some needed educational space. As part of the fund-raising program, I preached a three-week series on biblical stewardship. We discovered that the new believers from "Saturday Night" who attended the Sunday services were upset about the topic. They did not care about a building and felt I was wasting my preaching time. "We want to learn the Bible for our lives," they said. And some of them stopped coming on Sundays until the series was concluded.

Now, I thought I was teaching the Bible as it related to our facility needs. But *not* the new believers. I learned that new believers and unchurched people see things much differently from the old-timers, and we had better be sensitive to their concerns if we are to reach them.

"A MAP" Demands More Than Evangelism

"To win as many as possible" is more than evangelism. It involves at least three things centered in Jesus Christ: (1) trusting Christ—evangelism, (2) following Christ—edification, (3) serving Christ—involvement. We must be committed to evangelism, edification, and involvement.

Calvary Church has tried to flesh out these objectives into operational goals. These statements, while not perfect or complete, represent our attempt to define the overall mission of winning as many as possible:

1. Communicate the gospel in a culturally relevant way to every person in Grand Rapids and around the world (1 Cor. 9:22).
   a. Identify and pray for people groups.
   b. Train people for evangelism.
   c. Mobilize people by encouraging the development of ministries that will reach people for Christ.
   d. Provide public expressions of evangelism.
2. Encourage all believers in their unique journey toward spiritual maturity (Col. 1:28).
   a. Enable all believers to study, understand, and apply the Word of God (2 Tim. 2:15).
   b. Enable all believers to engage in a life of personal and community prayer (Heb. 4:16; Acts 4:31; Eph. 6:18–20; 1 Thess. 5:17).
   c. Enable all believers to worship God in Spirit and in truth (John 4:23).
   d. Enable all believers to identify with at least one small group within the church.
   e. Enable all believers to demonstrate the Lordship of Christ in every area of life (Rom. 12:1–2).
3. Enable all believers to discover and exercise their role through the ministries of the church.
   a. Help all believers to discover their spiritual giftedness (1 Cor. 12:7).
   b. Provide training for all believers to develop their spiritual giftedness.
   c. Mobilize all believers in areas of ministry connected to their spiritual giftedness.
4. Enable all believers to reproduce themselves in the lives of others (1 Tim. 2:2).
   a. Provide instruction and training in the principles of servant leadership (2 Tim. 3:16–17).
   b. Provide opportunities to mobilize people in areas of servant leadership (Matt. 28:18–20).

Over the past two years my wife and I have had the privilege of opening up our home to individuals who attended the "Saturday Night" service but had the desire to take another step through a small-group Bible study. The majority of individuals who have come are brand-new believers with lots of questions. Others include those who have not yet made a decision for Christ and those who made a decision way back when but lost their direction and want to find their way back.

We consider it a privilege to lead these weekly studies because we receive so much more than we give. The studies are very basic, which is essential because it is exactly what these new babes in Christ need—"milk." . . . Week after week we sit back and watch as the lights come on and glow of new understanding shows on their faces—an understanding of basic truths mixed with the power of the Holy Spirit illuminating Scripture and opening their hearts, some for the first time.

Last year a woman called inquiring about the study, and after a brief explanation she quickly said this wasn't for her. I simply challenged her to come once and, if she felt that way, to not come again. Well, she came and was strictly business. She came out of a very traditional religious background and held a high-level position at one of the leading *Fortune* 500 companies. She came back the following week and committed her life to Christ the third week. It was such a thrill to see her dig into each lesson and discover who Jesus is and why he came. I remember her saying, "Oh, I get it! Jesus wants to establish a relationship with me! I was always taught religion was rules and traditions."

In these studies we seek to pass along truth mixed with our own experiences in our journey with Christ, but we also seek to instill a perspective about ministry. The individuals in the Saturday night crowd can reach areas that Calvary Church never could. Their pulpit is the assembly line, banks, restaurants, construction sites, etc. For my wife and I the fulfillment of seeing God's work in individual lives is only part of the joy—seeing those individuals reach out to others in their own sphere of influence is where real excitement comes in.

—*Mitch (and Chris) Bakker*

CHAPTER 6

SEVEN STEPS TO PREPARE THE CHURCH

Not all traditional churches are ready for a seeker-sensitive service. Perhaps most are not. To impose this kind of a service on a church that is not prepared will prove fatal to the program and detrimental to the church. In reflecting on the experience of Calvary Church with "Saturday Night," I can clearly identify several steps of preparation.

Step 1: Understand the Culture of the Church

I am convinced that not every traditional church should have a seeker-sensitive service because the culture of the church would strangle it quickly. To prepare our congregation, I spent some time studying the history of Calvary Church. The church was founded in 1929 by Dr. M. R. DeHaan, who also founded the Radio Bible Class. From the beginning the church was already a "megachurch" with an attendance of about fifteen hundred. As I talked with people who had been in the church in its early years, I began listing the distinctives of Calvary:

1. *The centrality of the teaching of the Scriptures.*
2. *The priority of world evangelization.* (The church currently gives more than a million dollars annually to missions.)
3. *The importance of music in worship.* (John W. Peterson and Clair Hess were ministers of music, Don Wyrtzen was an elder, and Harold DeCou was the organist.)
4. *Use of media to communicate the gospel.* (Radio and television have long been important ministries.)
5. *A strong educational program for children and youth.*

6. *Multiple lay leadership.* (We are a lay-led, not a staff-led, ministry.)

7. *Innovation in reaching people for Christ.* (In the 1930s, we are told, we were the first church in the country to have Vacation Bible School; in the 1950s we began to use drama and cantatas for outreach.)

I was impressed with some of the innovations of the church. When the church began broadcasting on radio, many Christians in the community were critical because they felt that Satan controlled the air waves ("the prince of the power of the air"). When the church started Vacation Bible School, a student could get on a streetcar or a bus anywhere in Grand Rapids and ride free to the program at Calvary Church. Dr. Louis Paul Lehman, a long-time pastor, introduced drama, all-night gospel concerts, Sunday school contests, and other new programs. John W. Peterson introduced a "new" style of music through his compositions and cantatas.

When I presented the idea of "Saturday Night," I tied it to the long history of innovations. This was another step within the generally accepted culture of our church. It is important that the culture of a church be open to innovation and change. If it is not, it would be difficult to introduce a significant change without a fight.

Step 2: Teach Levels of Truth and Behavior

Truth is truth, but not all truth is equally important. Jesus Christ is the Son of God—that's truth. We should be baptized—that's truth as well. But baptism is not as important as the truth about the person of Jesus Christ. Several years ago I introduced a paradigm to better understand the different levels of truth. Truth can be divided into three categories: absolutes, convictions, and preferences.

1. Absolutes. Absolutes are the critical truths of the Christian faith—the fundamentals. To deny these truths is to deny the essence of Christianity. People who deny them are not Christian even though they may be religious. These truths include

- The deity of Christ
- His substitutionary death on the cross
- His bodily resurrection
- Salvation by grace through faith

These truths are absolutes because they relate directly to our eternal destiny.

2. *Convictions.* Convictions include what we believe based on our interpretation of the Bible in areas other than the absolutes. Some issues are the mode of baptism, eschatology, ecclesiology, and charismatic gifts. Sincere Christians disagree on these issues because they interpret the Bible differently, but these issues do not determine eternal destiny.

3. *Preferences.* Preferences are matters we believe or do that are not based directly on our interpretations of the Bible. These include dress code, hair length (ponytails) for men, musical style, and forms of worship. We practice these things, but they are not convictions; they are cultural preferences

This paradigm of truth has been very helpful in developing tolerance in our congregation. Whenever I talk about rock music on Saturday night, people know it is a preference. They may not like it—in fact, they may hate it. But it is not a conviction; it is a preference. We should be tolerant of the preferences of others. Unfortunately, many churches elevate their preferences and convictions into absolutes. They preach "God's will" in everything from salvation to hair style; everyone must conform to their way of thinking and behaving. When this happens, the church is *not* ready for or open to a seeker-sensitive service.

We must remember these levels of truth when dealing with new believers. In some churches, the first thing a convert is given is a list of dos and don'ts that are primarily preferences. Discipleship should focus on the absolutes first—teaching believers to love God and each other, which are the two greatest commandments. Then one can begin introducing convictions. The *least* important thing is cultural preferences.

I know many people who came to Christ and were confused and hurt by the way they were treated:

"Get your hair cut."

"You can't wear shorts in this church."

"Quit smoking."

"Don't listen to rock music."

"We don't do that here."

Etc., etc., etc.

Churches that magnify preferences should avoid the seeker-sensitive approach to ministry. In my opinion, they should stay out of evangelism altogether. This kind of religious legalism is destructive, not constructive. Jesus said, "Woe to you, teachers of the law and Pharisees, you hypocrites! You travel over land and sea to win a single convert, and when he becomes one, you make him twice as much a son of hell as you are" (Matt. 23:15).

Step 3: Develop a System That Helps People Without a Lot of Preconditions

From the perspective of an objective observer, churches must seem rather paradoxical at times. We preach a salvation of grace without human effort: "All you need to do is trust Christ; you don't work for salvation." Then when people trust Christ, we hand them a voluminous list of what they must do.

I find this paradox in the questions some Christians ask about "Saturday Night":

How many come Sunday morning?

How many get baptized?

How many join the church?

My answers may seem shocking:

How many come Sunday morning? I don't know and I don't care. Our objective is not to use "Saturday Night" as a conduit to Sunday morning. If the people who attend "Saturday Night" never come on Sunday, that's okay.

How many get baptized? Some people get baptized, but we do not demand that. We are more interested in new believers' getting grounded in the Bible and growing spiritually than in being baptized. Eventually many of them get baptized, but there is no pressure to do it.

How many join the church? Not many. Membership is not an important issue to them or to us. To pressure them toward membership after they receive Christ would very likely turn them off and away from the church.

If you want to start a seeker-sensitive service, do not have a long list of expectations to impose on converts. If you feel compelled to have them attend on Sunday, get baptized, or become members immediately, you will probably drive them away. We have chosen to allow God to lead people as to when they are ready to make these choices. The same is true of dress, behavior, and other externals. If these become preconditions for acceptance, people will stop coming.

Step 4: Affirm Everyone in Ministry

You are all sons of God through faith in Christ Jesus, for all of you who were baptized into Christ have clothed yourselves with Christ. There is neither Jew nor Greek, slave nor free, male nor female, for you are all one in Christ Jesus. If you belong to Christ, then you are Abraham's seed, and heirs according to the promise (Gal. 3:26–28).

As evangelicals we loudly affirm Paul's statement about "oneness" in Christ. We believe that religious, social, and sexual differences are essentially moot issues in the family of God. However, when it comes to living out this principle in the culture of our churches, we do not do so well. Consider the general role of women in church ministries:

Often their role is secondary and performed in relative obscurity; they do not usher, pray, speak, or lead.

As we started "Saturday Night," we decided to change that pattern. We included and affirmed women at every level of the seeker service. Women head up major committees connected to the service. They usher, lead in prayer, read Scripture, give the talk, and answer questions. This is different from our customary Sunday pattern (which we are in the process of changing). We want the unchurched people who attend "Saturday Night" to see in visible ways that we affirm *all* people in ministry.

This cultural affirmation of men and women is an important ingredient in "Saturday Night," and I also believe it is important in developing any seeker-sensitive service.

Step 5: Maintain Total Commitment

Starting a seeker-sensitive service requires a total commitment. A half-hearted commitment is the seed of failure, as many traditional churches have learned. What do I mean by total commitment?

1. The involvement of the senior pastor. A seeker-sensitive service is very likely to be the most controversial ministry in a traditional church. For this reason it must have the involvement—not just the support—of the senior pastor. I want people at Calvary Church to know that when they criticize "Saturday Night," they are criticizing *me.* I want them to know that I am involved in the planning, promotion, oversight, and speaking for "Saturday Night."

2. The seeker service is just as important as the Sunday worship. A seeker-sensitive service cannot be a second-class citizen. It must be organized and treated as important as any Sunday service or else it will become a "cute" little thing you do on the side.

3. Other activities must be scheduled around the service. Holding the seeker service in our auditorium meant we could no longer schedule Saturday night weddings. In fact, we do not allow any wedding after 1:00 P.M. on Saturday because we need the afternoon to set up the platform. No other church ministry or activity can replace or preempt "Saturday Night."

4. *Financial support.* It takes money to run a seeker service, especially for advertising. Calvary Church has been generous in its funding of "Saturday Night."

5. *Flexibility in recruiting of personnel.* "Saturday Night" requires a lot of volunteers and a lot *from* the volunteers. We do not expect these volunteers to spend all day Sunday in church as well. You need to encourage those who make a seeker service effective to feel free to stay home for part of Sunday. This may seem a foreign idea in a traditional church setting, but people who try to "do it all" will quickly burn out.

6. *Enthusiastic support of the board.* Church boards tolerate a lot, but if its support of a seeker service is merely tolerance, you will probably encounter problems. It is important that the board give enthusiastic support.

Step 6: Retain Long-Term Openness

A seeker service is a long-term commitment. Many times we have considered dropping "Saturday Night," usually amid uncertainty caused by a major drop in attendance or a slower rate of growth than the Sunday services. Sunday morning attendance at Calvary grew from 2,500 to nearly 5000 in the first four years of "Saturday Night." The seeker-service attendance fluctuated greatly and leveled off at about 800.

We have learned not to compare these attendance figures. We have learned to work through the cycles of change and not flag in our commitment.

Step 7: Stay Flexible

To start a seeker service, you need flexibility and tolerance in the congregation, and flexibility in the program itself. We continually evaluate and change what we are doing. The church has given us that flexibility. We do not have to check with twenty committees when we make a change; we have the freedom to do what is needed.

The ability to adapt quickly is important to a seeker-sensitive service. To delay changes for months would be detrimental to the health and growth of the ministry. Therefore it is necessary for the board to entrust that ministry to the people who are closest to it. To control it with a "system" does not work.

I was raised in a Christian home by a very loving family. Baptized as an infant, I attended church and Sunday school regularly. I also had the opportunity to attend a Christian school for thirteen years. I was read Bible stories and learned memory verses for as long as I can remember. I made Profession of Faith when I was sixteen years old, which means I stood in front of the congregation and acknowledged Jesus Christ as Lord of my life. My life as a Christian was routine and simple. To the outsider, it would appear that I had done all the right things.

The routine went on, but I began to feel a need for something more in my life—something stable, something to trust and rely on, a source of direction. I had a strong sense that this would come from church. But who was I to go to church for direction? After all, I attended church twice on Sunday. I knew all kinds of verses. I prayed when I needed to. I knew God—what else could be missing?

Well, I found that answer in a small-group Bible study. All the years of stories and verses in my head did not make a bit of difference. What I saw in the other women in the group was that I was missing a heartfelt love of God, a total commitment of my daily life to him. I recognized that I had been running my life my way. Sure, Christ was in it, but I wasn't relying on him. My life was hectic, stressful, and unfulfilling. I asked Christ to take control of my life, and the reality of his awesome love is present daily in my life now. I now realize what was missing. I have taken twenty-five years of head knowledge and moved it into my heart. I live each day in the peace of knowing I am a child of God and not a hair falls from my head without him knowing. I now have someone to trust and rely on, and I have a source for direction in my life.

I realize that sharing Christ with others does not take a lot of knowledge, but an unconditional love, like Christ had. I desire to share the personal relationshiop that I have with Christ with others. Realizing the love of God in my heart and giving daily control of my life to him has made all the difference.

—Sandy Haga

CHAPTER 7

BEHIND THE SCENES

Saturday Night is more than a service that occurs on Saturday evenings between 6:00 and 7:15. Behind the scenes there is a multitude of activity, organization, and involvement from various people. This infrastructure is as important as the program itself, for without it, the seeker service could not function.

Ditch Diggers

The "Ditch Diggers" are volunteers who staff the Saturday service. They are recruited from both the Saturday and the Sunday congregations. The term comes from 2 Kings 3:16–17

> And he said, "This is what the LORD says: Make this valley full of ditches. For this is what the LORD says: You will see neither wind nor rain, yet this valley will be filled with water, and you, your cattle and your other animals will drink."

Before God provided water in Israel, the people had to dig ditches all over the valley. Once these ditches were dug, God sent adequate water to meet their needs. The "Saturday Night" Ditch Diggers likewise prepare the way, planning, organizing, and praying for the service. Often what they do is not glamorous, but it is vital so that the flow of "spiritual" water can continue unhindered.

We offer extensive training for the Ditch Diggers in evangelism, discipleship, servanthood, hospitality, and relating to unchurched people. The Ditch Diggers divide into small groups and rotate their functions every four weeks throughout the year. By year's end they have been involved in every aspect of ministry. It takes 37 Ditch Diggers every week to make "Saturday Night" work. Functions include stage set-up, lighting and sound, nursery, greeting, hospitality, ushering, counseling, and community relations.

In addition, there are more than 350 Ditch Diggers who pray for "Saturday Night." They have no direct involvement in the program, but make a commitment to pray daily for the service. We send a monthly prayer letter to these people. We give them stickers that say "Pray for Saturday Night." Their support is crucial.

Advertising

About 65 percent of the budget for "Saturday Night" is spent on advertising ($27,000 in 1992).

Billboards. We purchased one billboard sign that will appear in twelve different locations in the course of one year. It is a large, simple message that can be read quickly. Our surveys indicate that at least one-third of all the newcomers have seen the billboard many times.

Radio. We purchased radio time on the most-listened-to "light rock" station in the city. We have made commercials—everything from a man-on-the-street scene to rap— and find that their style and placement in secular media bring a great response. We do not buy time on traditional Christian radio stations because that is not the audience we are trying to reach.

Daily newspaper. We place one 4-x-6-inch ad each week on the movie page, again in the hope of attracting people who do not usually go to church. It is a "fast-read" type of ad that highlights the topic for the night. We run this ad only in Saturday's paper because we feel that for people who look at this page, "to come or not to come" is a strictly impulsive decision. The choice of topic, therefore, is extremely important.

Weekly papers. We have occasionally purchased ad space in the weekly publications, typical of most cities, called "On

The Town" or "Tonight in Grand Rapids." There appears to be only a moderate return on these ads because this medium is a hit-and-miss kind of promotion.

We also purchase ad space in some of the printed programs that are handed out at college athletic events. The synergy of this multimedia approach has proved to be quite effective.

Television. We have experimented three times with fifteen-second television ads on the local cable outlet and the local FOX network. These consist of fast-paced, one-word reactions to the question, "What do you think of 'Saturday Night'?" Then we flip up a date, time, and place for the last five seconds. These spots work extremely well when placed in programs like "Arsenio Hall" and Detroit Lions professional football games.

Posters, programs, and handouts. We have created two types of poster-handout items: one to carry in your pocket, the other to mail to friends or tack onto bulletin boards. We keep the size small so they will not be cumbersome for people to handle. We print several thousands of these at a time, place them on college bulletin boards, in student mailboxes (with permission of the college), and in the pew racks of the church.

Although we recognize that the best form of advertising is word of mouth, we still think it is important to use paid advertisements. In designing the budget for "Saturday Night," we accepted this premise from Madison Avenue: "To move a person to try any new product or idea for the first time, they must be exposed to that product or idea at least twenty times before they react." To reach the unchurched of our community with the idea of going to church, our advertising deserved repetition, saturation, and focus in those media to which these people are exposed most often.

This is the script for one radio commercial:

Radio Spot
"Saturday Night" . . . :60 sec.
September 1992

(Music up . . .) Oh Yeah! *(very up)*
Crowd sounds become obvious over music
Over music and crowd sounds, alien voice saying
"Saturday Night . . . Yes!" *(keeps repeating over and over)*
Crowd sounds (individual voices piercing through)

    (Man) "He keeps saying . . . Saturday Night"
    (Lady) "How does he know about that . . ."
    (Man) "Everybody knows about Saturday Night"
    (Lady) "Sure is funny looking . . . but very smart"
    (Man) "I knew Saturday Night was out of this world,
            but . . ."
    (Lady) "He sure knows a good thing . . ."
  (Official) "All right, folks . . . what's the problem? . . .
            let's break it up . . ."
    (Lady) "But, sir, look what we've found . . ."
  (Official) "Hey, my little marshmallow kind of buddy . . .
            you're a long way from home aren't you? . . .
            and you've heard about Saturday Night . . . Oh,
            I get it . . . you wanna know what it's all about
            my little puffball . . .

            Well, it's music that kicks . . .
            With drama with clicks . . .
            And real people shed light
            With talks that are just right
            It's new friends, not chancers
            There's questions and answers
            So . . . Come as you are . . .
            Be you look or gawker . . .
            It's for people like you
            And a little cloud walker . . .

"Saturday Night" . . . it's out of this world
Every week . . . six o'clock
Calvary Church, I-96 and East Beltline

"This week we're exploring the world of _____"
(Music . . .) "Oh yeah!"

Singles Viewpoint

Between 50 and 60 percent of the people who attend "Saturday Night" are single, and we have worked hard to respond to their needs. One means is a program entitled "Singles Viewpoint." This began in the fall of 1990 after some singles expressed a desire to meet as an affinity group after the regularly scheduled "Saturday Night" program. The original idea was to offer a "Talk It Over" format for single adults, but the idea evolved through several stages in becoming "Singles Viewpoint."

Phase one. About twelve leaders were recruited and trained to lead small-group discussions on the topic addressed in "Saturday Night." Discussions took place at round tables set up in the church fellowship hall.

At first, about fifty single adults participated in "Talk It Over" and the free sandwich supper that came with it. Some groups clicked, others did not. Some groups were seen laughing and appearing to have a wonderful time—they returned week by week. Others were quiet and looked rather miserable—they never returned. Few people knew one another. The random, spontaneous discussion groups did not work well. By the end of November 1990, the number of people participating had dropped to twenty-five or thirty each week. "Talk It Over" was all talked out.

Phase two. Still believing that single adults needed to meet after "Saturday Night," we tried an open forum. Instead of having discussion in small groups, the speaking took on a "town meeting" appearance. The discussion time was led by a group facilitator using the written questions that did not get covered in "Saturday Night." Additional material on the topic of the evening was included. "Talk It Over" began to grow as single adults felt more comfortable with the large-group format. The room was still arranged with round tables, and the supper was still provided, enabling singles to meet others in an informal setting.

Phase three. One week featured a guest "expert" on the evening's subject. The facilitator interviewed the guest and invited singles to ask questions. Then the discussion took an interesting shift: The guest did not answer one particular question, but turned it back to the audience, asking, "What do you think?" A lively discussion of opinions and feelings developed. It was as if such a simple idea was waiting to be developed all along. It was almost like the "Phil Donahue" show. That was it! A talk-show format with the audience not only asking questions, but giving their own opinions and viewpoints.

Over the next few weeks we experimented with a variety of formats, room arrangements, and special guests. Doug Fagerstrom, the singles pastor at Calvary, had been moderating the program, and then Jenny Shell was added as a co-host. Her perspectives were sometimes uniquely different from Doug's. Jenny was able to stimulate dialogues with the singles as only another single adult could. Thus the program offered two viewpoints, to which the audience could add more.

The "Donahue" format won out. Attendance grew rapidly to exceed one hundred, sometimes reaching two hundred.

At present, guests include single adults sharing their own experiences and experts who have been trained in particular fields such as medicine, sexuality, or finances. We have found that panels of two or three persons work much better than four or five, because we allow only forty-five minutes for the program after a half-hour supper.

The topic for "Singles Viewpoint" is no longer the same as at "Saturday Night." We have found it simply does not need to be the same. But the issues are relevant. These were the topics for winter 1992 (see also appendix D):

Sexuality, part I: Bed or breakfast?
Sexuality, part II: What are the real consequences?
Death: Facing others and yours
Having an affair: What attracts singles to marrieds?
Having an affair: How to break the bond
Date rape: Prevention

Date rape: Healing from the memory
My rights: Censorship, what can I see or say?

Evangelism and Discipleship

When people make a commitment to Christ at a seeker-sensitive service, it is important to provide small-group or one-on-one discipleship. We like to offer several options, such as these group experiences:

Greenhouse. On Sunday mornings at 8:30, Jim and Mary Zuidema lead a discussion group for new believers, where they pursue the struggles and issues of Christian living. People seeking answers to tough questions are rooted and encouraged in their faith. Jim and Mary also attend "Saturday Night" and are recognized there so that inquirers can meet with them afterward to talk or pray. That helps to establish a relationship. Jim and Mary invite these people to Greenhouse or introduce them to a Greenhouse member for personal follow-up.

Seed. Seed is stage two. Led by Mitch and Chris Bakker, Seed meets on Sunday mornings at 8:30 and focuses on sharing one's faith and discipling others. Both the Zuidemas and Bakkers have a network of mature believers who can personally disciple converts. This network is the heart and soul of establishing new believers in the faith. Every week I meet with a new believer and begin working through the discipleship materials of the Navigators organization.

Bible study. On Sunday evenings we offer an eight-week introductory study on the meaning of Christianity. We usually have two groups meeting simultaneously. We advertise them at "Saturday Night." Of the fifteen or so people in each group, nearly half are nonbelievers.

Wednesday night. We believe that part of spiritual growth is worshiping with other believers in an environment where the focus is the teaching of the Scriptures. We discovered that many "Saturday Night" people who come on Sunday either get lost in the crowd or do not relate to the traditional setting. So we started a special Wednesday evening service. I offer the same sermon as Sunday night, but the service is more informal and casual. The attendance is about 400, of whom about half come to "Saturday Night." We also have Awana which is a children's program, and youth programs so that entire families can be ministered to.

My first reaction when I was asked to give my testimony was "I'm not ready," but one of my friends said that if I can do the job I do on a daily basis, I can share what Jesus Christ has done for me. I'm a police officer. I've been in foot pursuits, fights, and have been shot at. I also spent ten months working undercover, purchasing cocaine. I guess if I can handle that, I can certainly tell why Jesus Christ has made such an impact on my life.

I was saved through a church youth group at age seven. I grew up in a very loving and Christian home, but no one ever showed me what it was like to have a personal relationship with Jesus Christ. I never knew how to make Christ the center of my life or let him control my life.

I made it through college, began my career, got married, and had a child. I thought my life was going along just great. Shortly after my daughter was born, my husband and I quit communicating, and three years of emotional abuse began. I lost my identity and self-esteem. At that time I was the only female member of a fifteen-member tactical team—or S.W.A.T., for a more glorious term. I was "one of the boys." . . .

During this time, my husband began a relationship with someone else. I chose to look the other way because I didn't want to believe it. I was desparately trying to hold my marriage together. The whole time I felt my life getting more and more out of control. I knew I needed to get Christ back at the center of my life, so I started coming to Calvary Church and searching for the answers. But I didn't know how or where to start. Eventually my husband wanted out. It hit me that I was facing life and raising a three-year-old on my own. I was scared to death. So I did the only thing I knew how to do: I cried out to God for help. . . .

In Greenhouse I couldn't get enough of what I was hearing. I began to learn and memorize God's Word and how to apply it to my life. For the first time in three years I knew that I had value because I was a child of God and that Jesus loves me unconditionally. Also, no matter what mistakes I've made, he forgives me. I know I have God's strength. Now I know I can make it. I look forward to every new day, knowing that he is with me and I have a future with him.
                                                                    —*Cathy Quist*

CHAPTER 8

SEEKER SERVICES
IN A SMALLER SETTING

Not every church can budget $50,000 a year for a seeker-sensitive service. Not every congregation has the musical and dramatic talent needed for such a program. How do smaller churches with limited resources accomplish this kind of evangelistic outreach? The answer lies in applying the principles of seeker ministry, not in imitating the details of a particular program.

Perhaps the most important principle is to relate the gospel in a culturally relevant way to unchurched people. This involves both contact with the unchurched and a sensitivity to communicate the gospel in acceptable and understandable terms.

Seeker-Sensitive at a Personal Level

Being seeker-sensitive begins at a personal level. We do not have to have a *program* to be seeker-sensitive; we begin by being in contact with unchurched people. And herein lies the problem. Many laypeople and their pastors are self-limiting in their association with the unchurched. Many Christians spend most of their time around other believers. In fact, many programs in our churches promote this separation: Christian day school, Christian aerobic classes, Christian softball leagues, etc., etc., etc. The sum total of all this activity is to isolate churchgoers from the rest of society. The result is that we lose contact with people who need the Lord.

I have worked hard not to become isolated. Because my wife is actively involved in the public school system, we have invited teachers, other parents, administrators, and board members to outreach events connected with our church. I run at an athletic club several days a week, and I try to build relationships with the unchurched people I meet there.

Playing soccer in a summer league puts me around people who curse and swear, but I persist because it is an outreach opportunity. When our street has a block party, we go—we don't bring or drink the beer, but we go. We invite neighbors to our home to try to build relationships to talk about Christ.

Many Christians do not think this way. They dislike being around people who smoke or drink or curse. They are wary of inviting unchurched people into their homes: "They might light up a cigarette, you know." They would rather play sports in church leagues and be around Christians *all* the time. Such an approach to life eliminates most opportunities for evangelism.

I am convicted by the model of Christ in regard to personal evangelism.

> While Jesus was having dinner at Matthew's house, many tax collectors and "sinners" came and ate with him and his disciples. When the Pharisees saw this, they asked his disciples, "Why does your teacher eat with tax collectors and 'sinners'?" On hearing this, Jesus said, "It is not the healthy who need a doctor, but the sick. But go and learn what this means: 'I desire mercy, not sacrifice.' For I have not come to call the righteous, but sinners" (Matt. 9:10–13).

> Now the tax collectors and "sinners" were all gathering around to hear him. But the Pharisees and the teachers of the law muttered, "This man welcomes sinners and eats with them." Then Jesus told them this parable: "Suppose one of you has a hundred sheep and loses one of them. Does he not leave the ninety-nine in the open country and go after the lost sheep until he finds it? And when he finds it, he joyfully puts it on his shoulders and goes home. Then he calls his friends and neighbors together and says, 'Rejoice with me; I have found my lost sheep.' I tell you that in the same way there will be more rejoicing in heaven over one sinner who repents than over ninety-nine righteous persons who do not need to repent" (Luke 15:1–7).

Do I eat with "publicans and sinners"? Do I attend pagan parties? Do people accuse me of being a friend to people outside the church? If your calendar is filled exclusively with appointments with other Christians, you are not following the model of Jesus. It is natural for Christians to associate with other Christians, for they share the same Savior and the same values. It requires diligent effort and radical choices not to exclude the outside world from our circles of interest and concern.

Seeker-Sensitive in the Ministries of the Church

Devoting a major weekend service to seekers is not the only way to develop programs for the unchurched. A church of limited resources still has many options in evangelism. "Saturday Night" is only one of the many ministries of Calvary Church intended for meeting people where they are.

1. Backyard Bible Clubs. For many years we held Daily Vacation Bible School. We encouraged young people to come to the church building for one week in August for crafts, songs, Scripture stories, and the gospel. Then we made a major change in our focus and took the program out into the community. We now have about forty Backyard Bible Clubs during the same week in August. The opportunities to reach unchurched children and their families have multiplied because we are out where the needs are. Anytime we can shift evangelism outside the walls of the church and into the community, we can more effectively attract the unchurched.

2. Christmas and Easter programs. Nearly all churches have special musical and dramatic programs to celebrate Christmas and Easter. Six years ago Calvary Church decided to make these evangelistic. We encourage people to invite nonbelieving friends to attend. Toward the end of the program, I take ten minutes to relate the gospel and give people an opportunity to receive Christ by praying silently where they are sitting. A card in the program enables people to indicate a spiritual need, a desire to talk with someone, or a decision to receive Christ. We have small-group Bible studies to follow-up with converts.

3. Support groups. People who live in the trenches of ministry are increasingly aware of the pain of others. I believe emotional and physical pain are divine strategies to get people's attention. For that reason we offer a number of support groups for people who struggle in different ways:

New Leaf: For men struggling with sexual desires

H.I.S.: For women to provide help for survivors of sexual abuse

Mending Hearts: For women to offer comfort to those who have lost a loved one through death

Loving Support: For women who live with or love someone who has abused alcohol

Dealing with Grief and Loss: For single adults who have lost a mate or loved one to death

Employment Transitions: For single and other adults to focus on constructive ideas to help them through this time of transition

Adult Children of Alcoholics: For adult children of alcoholics or similarly dysfunctional families

Young Single Moms: For young, never-married mothers

Divorce Recovery Workshop: Follow-up support for participants in the eight-week Divorce Recovery Workshop series that the church offers three times a year

Big Buddy: For children of single parents to provide them with models of care and nurture

Mental Illness Family Support: For people suffering from the effects of serious mental illness in the family

It is important that support groups move people beyond their struggles into a personal relationship with Christ. We do not substitute spiritual growth for "self-help" principles. It is critical that group leaders place a priority on bringing people to Christ and encouraging them on their spiritual journey.

Alcoholics Anonymous and Narcotics Anonymous groups use the church facilities also. The leaders are members of Calvary Church. Even though these groups are not directly evangelistic, the leaders encourage the participants to attend the Saturday or Sunday services.

Support groups offer a way to be seeker-sensitive, but they sometimes draw criticism. We have been accused of giving up on the Bible, ignoring Christ, and offering psychology as the answer to life problems. We have been accused of letting outside groups use our building who do not share our biblical conscience. Nevertheless, we persist in spite of the criticism.

4. Divorce Recovery Workshops. If we believe that the gospel offers forgiveness and a new beginning, then people who have endured the nightmare of divorce need to hear this good news. Three times a year we hold Divorce Recovery Workshops consisting of eight weekly meetings. They include lectures and small-group discussion. "Club Rainbow" is a program for the children whose parents are in the workshop.

The last night of the workshop we share the gospel. A recent trend is that many from the Divorce Recovery Workshops have started attending "Saturday Night" as a second step in their spiritual journey.

5. Campus Safari. This is an annual outreach of junior and senior high school students. The program is held in a gym on Sunday morning, lasts for two hours, and includes music, gymnastics, martial arts, testimonies, and the sharing of the gospel. There are competitions based on the schools represented.

6. Home Bible studies. A good nonthreatening way to talk about the gospel is through inviting unchurched people to home-based Bible studies. We call them "Discovery Groups." These are six-week introductory studies to the Christian faith. As many as 60 percent of the participants are nonbelievers.

7. *Personal evangelism.* The most effective strategy for reaching the unchurched is by the personal contact of believers with nonbelievers within their circles of influence. There is no formal program, no organizational structure, and no budget—just people sharing their faith with others.

A Seeker-Sensitive Service

Can a church with limited resources have an effective seeker service? Absolutely! It may not be held every week, it may not have a live band, it may not have a neon sign—but it can be done. Consider these ideas:

Do not hold it every week. At least, do not attempt a weekly service at the outset. Begin by planning one service. If it is beneficial, then try it again several months later. You may find that a monthly schedule is better for your church than weekly services.

Choose a relevant topic. Appendix C contains a long list of topics. Choose a topic that unchurched people will identify with and one that you will be comfortable addressing.

Do not fret if there is no live band. Taped music can be used to accompany a singer. Videos of contemporary artists are available. Both approaches offer quality music.

Recruit and train the drama people. You might be surprised who in the congregation have performed in drama in high school or college. Cultivate that interest and build on their experience. Choose drama that relates to the topic of the service.

Have someone to share a testimony. It is more important that people are enthusiastic about their relationship to Christ than that they are public speakers. Some people at "Saturday Night" read their testimonies. Sincerity is more important than speech principles.

Use video. If videos are available, use them. They can greatly enhance the program because we have an increasingly visual-oriented society.

Focus on church members' inviting others. You do not need an advertising budget if people are faithful in spreading the news by word of mouth. If people will invite their friends, you will have a crowd.

Provide refreshments afterward. Food and eating provide an informal setting for people to meet others.

After a wedding at which I officiated, a person came up to me and asked the "nightmare" question, "Hi, do you remember me?" I confessed that I did not.

"I talked to you four years ago after a Saturday night service." He said that God gave him a vision that night of arranging a similar service in his community on a Saturday night. He met with more than one hundred pastors to ask their support, and they all declined, but he forged ahead. Three years later he saw the first service held. The group now rents a Salvation Army auditorium every Saturday night for music, drama, and a "testimonial." The talk consists of someone's sharing a personal testimony.

"It's incredible," the man said. "Thanks for motivating me to see what could be done in our town."

My family started out going to church because my mother's father was a minister. We stopped going because all of us kids got too hard to handle. But I knew about God and feared him.

I had a lot of accidents while growing up: A horse kicked me in the head, I got cut up by the lawnmower, and I shot myself in the leg by accident. I used to ask God why all of these things were happening to me. My father used to drink a lot and scare me because he was verbally abusive. I grew up with a complex in school. I had a problem making friends because I was a bully.

When I got older I started fighting all the time at the bars to release the stress that my ex-girlfiend and the business put on me. . . . I got thrown in jail for smashing a windshield out of a car. While I was in jail I would go to church and sing and pray. I started to slow way down when I got out of jail, . . . but I was sick of my patterns. I did not want to go on this way. The monster that lived inside of me had to be destroyed. I asked God if this was the end of my life. He had given me incredible talents, and I didn't understand why I felt this was the end of my life. I got down on my knees and asked God to help me out.

The next thing I knew, I was at a "Saturday Night" listening to Ed Dobson talk about forgiveness. I spoke with a counselor about my problems. I went on feeling bad, trying to figure this out, when one of my business vendors asked me if I wanted tickets to Calvary's Easter program. I went and took a friend. As soon as I sat down, I started crying. My past life flashed up in front of me like it was on a movie screen. As I saw Jesus being punished in the play, I recalled what the counselor had said about growing up without getting filled up inside.

All of a sudden I felt the left side of my chest start to expand. I started to feel a peace and questioned if the Holy Spirit was filling me up. The feeling came on stronger. The love of Jesus Christ had entered my heart. For the first time, I could forgive people, including my father. I was at total peace with myself.

—James D. Frisbie

CHAPTER 9

WHAT WE ARE LEARNING

The experience with a seeker service at Calvary Church has been a pilgrimage of growth and change. My initial title for this chapter was "What We Have Learned," but that suggests we have stopped learning and have arrived. This is not true. We continue to learn. We do not have all the answers. Sometimes I am not sure we even know all the questions, but we try to remain open and adaptable. After five years, these are some of the lessons we have learned.

Do Not Mix Traditional and Seeker Services

"Saturday Night" is radical: drama, rock music, live band, lights, neon sign, bright banners, blue jeans. Sunday morning is not radical: choir, orchestra, praise chorus, hymns, pastoral prayer, suit and tie.

Other church leaders have observed what we do on Saturday and like it. They return to their churches, change a few things on Sunday morning to be more contemporary, and in almost every case meet opposition and dissension. We have learned that Saturday and Sunday are separate services and *cannot* be mixed. If you try to combine them, you ruin both.

One Sunday afternoon, after about a year of "Saturday Night," I was going over the sermon for the evening service. The musicians were rehearsing the special music—a small vocal group accompanied by a live band, with drums, bass guitar, and brass. The band was practicing the offertory. It was contemporary, hot, and *far* beyond what we had ever done on a Sunday.

Before the service I told the minister of music that I

thought the musical package was too much in one service and was probably beyond what the church could tolerate on a Sunday night. But we went ahead with it. Most of the congregation loved it, but those who did not were very vocal.

For weeks we answered complaints, met with people, responded to the board, and heard why we should not have had that music. I discovered that the smallest changes on Sunday stir volatile feelings among the same people who tolerate something more on Saturday night. Saturday and Sunday don't mix.

We have also learned to exercise restraint at "Saturday Night." *Any* attempt to impose what we do on Sunday is rejected. We had a four-week survey of the Bible, which I thought people would enjoy. Instead, we dropped about three hundred in attendance over the series. It was too much like Sunday.

The point is restraint, restraint, restraint. You cannot mix traditional and seeker-sensitive services. You do not make a traditional service seeker-sensitive by playing a few contemporary tunes or having drama or not wearing a tie. A seeker-sensitive service is a separate entity, and you ruin that entity by shifting it into a traditional mold.

The Seeker Service Has Become a Church Within a Church

To people who attend our traditional services on Sunday, "Saturday Night" is a "program." To those who come on Saturday night, it is *not* a program—it is their church. There are several reasons why. First, people consider "Saturday Night" a worship service. Many who have grown up in a traditional environment dismiss the idea that "Saturday Night" is worship. Even I did so for quite a while. Then I was challenged by the question, "What do you do on "Saturday Night?" My response was, "Drama, music, Scripture reading, prayer, testimony, talk, question-and-answer time." The person responded, "That sounds like worship to me." For those who attend "Saturday Night" regularly, it is.

Second, "Saturday Night" has become in essence a

separate church within Calvary Church. I first recognized this while I was at a local hospital. When I entered the elevator, one of the two people already there said, "We come to Calvary every week."

"Great!" I said.

"We love it," they said. They disclosed that they come on Saturday night; they do not attend on Sunday or midweek— only on Saturday. Yet they consider themselves a part of Calvary Church—and just as much a part as those who attend on Sunday.

We struggle with the long-term future of "Saturday Night," because we do not know whether we should continue with this church within Calvary. Should we "turn it loose" as a new church? We are not sure. But we are committed long-term to seeing it grow and develop.

A Seeker Service Takes More Work
Than the Traditional Services

I believe we spend more time and energy on the one hour and ten minutes of "Saturday Night" than all four of the traditional services on Sunday. My training and background is in traditional church ministry. "Saturday Night" has moved me out of my comfort zone and has therefore demanded significant effort and energy to minister in what is primarily a foreign context.

Planning energy. A seeker service demands careful planning. We choose the topics months in advance. We spend much time turning those topics into titles for each week. Then we plan the drama to coordinate with the topics. We look for music, Christian and secular, that speaks to these topics. All this is just the initial planning stage.

Preparation energy. I spend eight to ten hours a week preparing the talk. This preparation is radically different from studying the Bible in order to give verse-by-verse exposition. I read many secular magazines and popular books to prepare for Saturday, and little theology or religion. When I go to the Bible I ask myself the question, "What should I say about this verse assuming that people are hearing it for the first time?" I can take nothing for granted.

Execution energy. Execution energy begins every Saturday afternoon at two o'clock when the stage crew arrives to put up the set. The band rehearses from 3:00 to 4:00 P.M. Then the drama is rehearsed. At 4:30, we run through the entire program, without the talk. This allows time to work out the sound, the lights, and the cues. At 5:15, we eat a light meal together, followed by a time of prayer. So when we start the service at six o'clock, most of the people involved have been at the church for three or four hours already. Then the service starts.

Follow-up energy. After the service, I usually talk to several people about their problems. Others lead small groups or meet with people one-on-one. This requires energy. By the time the evening's events are over, the people who make "Saturday Night" work have been at church for five or six hours of intense ministry. This pace of ministry has proved to be very draining. We have encouraged many who assist on Saturday to reduce or eliminate their attendance on Sunday.

A Seeker Service Will Probably Be Misunderstood and Criticized

Hugh, the minister of music at Calvary, lectured at a Christian college on what we are doing at "Saturday Night." In a question time, one person said, "I think what you are doing is just worldly," and quoted a string of verses about separation and worldliness.

Hugh responded, "Now which part of the service do you consider worldly?" The person replied, "All of it!"

I had a similar experience. A week after I spoke at a Christian college about creative, nontraditional ministries, a prominent Bible expositor spoke there and castigated me. He declared that unless you teach the Bible in an expository way, you do not really have biblical ministry. (Of course, there are no examples in the Bible of expository, verse-by-verse sermons.)

Seeker services can become the focal point of criticism in the Christian community. Our church has been accused of compromise. We have been accused of using worldly or satanic music. We have been accused of giving up the Bible. We have been criticized as being weak on sin. We have been accused of a commitment to entertainment, not ministry. We have been called lenient toward homosexuality and other lifestyle choices. We have been criticized because the people who attend do not carry Bibles.

At times I become angry toward the critics and want to defend myself and the church. But arguing about these matters is generally useless. Therefore I have chosen to ignore the criticisms. The church supports "Saturday Night." I feel secure that we have not violated the Bible, and I know we will answer to God, not Christians.

It Is Easier to Start a New Church Than to Change a Traditional One

Change is a painful process that usually meets resistance in people. It requires great diligence, patience, and persistence to initiate the changes necessary to conduct a seeker service. Many traditional churches have tried and failed. It is much easier to start a new church on seeker principles.

I have mentioned that I am disappointed at the rate of numerical growth of "Saturday Night." I wish I could put *all* my energy and effort into the seeker service. I wish all the programs of the church supported and were committed to "Saturday Night." But they are not and never will be.

I have had to accept the reality that my time and energy are divided between a nontraditional church and a traditional church that meet in the same building and share the same resources. This division of time and energy is a limitation that all traditional churches will face if they initiate seeker-sensitive services.

I started out believing in God and knowing that He existed. I grew up in a church. However, I didn't understand that I could talk to God personally. I had said prayers, but it never really seemed that He was right there, that He was real. . . .

As I look back, I was really searching for something, as many kids do, especially in their high school years. I looked to my friends around me to give me that meaning. . . . I started looking to men for meaning, thinking that relationships were the key thing. I started dating a guy that would soon be my husband. However, he wasn't a Christian. I never really put a major emphasis on that because obviously I wasn't living a Christian life. . . . When the storms of marriage came, I just didn't know where to turn because my husband was my life. When there came a wedge between us, I was left alone again and still searching.

So I started looking for meaning in a job. I thought that if I had a job that made me feel important, that would give me meaning in my life. That didn't work either. Eventually I ended up having an affair with someone I worked with. Needless to say, that ended my marriage. I often think that Satan meant that whole situation for evil, but God used it for good because through it He created a hunger in me to know Him better. . . . I came to the realization that I needed more in my life. . . .

I had heard about Calvary Church and I went there one Sunday. . . . I was a little uneasy and not sure what to do, so I went to "Saturday Night" one time. It was just a really neat service. It was something I could relate to—the skits hit me between the eyes. I knew that I had found a little bit of what I was searching for, so I decided to get involved in a Sunday school class and picked up a "Singles Edition" on Saturday night and then noticed the Greenhouse class. . . .

It's been a little over a year and a half now since I started this journey, and I found that God has really filled my life. He has changed my life dramatically. I am thankful for all that He has done for me.
                                                              —*Anne Lawrence*

CHAPTER 10

THE MOST FREQUENTLY ASKED QUESTIONS ABOUT SEEKER SERVICES

*D*uring the last two years there have been several small church groups at each "Saturday Night" service. These groups came from churches all over the Midwest to observe our seeker-sensitive service and to try to develop similar services back home. I meet with these groups after the service to answer questions. From those interchanges, I have compiled a list of the most frequently asked questions about "Saturday Night." My answers seek to reflect what we have learned from our experiences.

Question 1: What is the most important prerequisite for starting a seeker service?
The most important requirement is a passion for evangelism. Unfortunately, this passion for evangelism is in serious decline in the evangelical community, partly because in many cases evangelical churches have become cloistered, monastic communities. They have lost touch with the real world. We tend to place our children in Christian day schools, develop our own church athletic programs, and spend most of our time with fellow believers. Therefore we get out of touch with the needs of the world that is outside of Christ. The idea of a seeker service can be threatening because it shifts us out of our comfort zone. I advise churches that have been isolated from the real world to proceed with a seeker service cautiously and prayerfully.

Question 2: How do we start?
First, you must have a clear sense of direction from the Lord that this is indeed what he is leading you to do. Second, examine the passion for evangelism within the leadership of

101

the church. If there is little passion for outreach, it will be very difficult to have a seeker service. Third, gather a small group of people who have a high level of commitment to seeing this happen. Begin exploring the idea with the objective of making a detailed report to the church board. This should include what you intend to do, how you intend to do it, what it will cost, who will be involved, when you will do it, and so on. Beginning a seeker service is not something a single person can do; it must become the vision of a group of people large enough to ensure that it happens.

Question 3: How many people from "Saturday Night" attend church on Sunday?
Some people want to gauge the success of "Saturday Night" directly by the number who also come on Sunday. We have chosen not to evaluate Saturday on that criterion. We are far more interested in people coming to personal faith in Christ, getting connected to a small group for spiritual growth, and then sharing their faith with others. Whether that happens on Saturday, Sunday, or any other day of the week is immaterial. We are satisfied when spiritual growth is occurring even if none of the people on "Saturday Night" show up on Sunday. Most do not attend on Sunday. Some do and eventually quit coming on Saturday night.

Question 4: What about follow-up?
It is very important to get people connected to small groups where they will sense personal concern and a level of accountability for their spiritual growth. This happens in different ways at Calvary. Some people get involved in one of the groups that meet after "Saturday Night" (such as Singles Viewpoint, Narcotics Anonymous, and small-group studies). Others take part in Sunday night home Bible studies. Many come to personal faith in Christ after joining a group. Still others get involved in the "Greenhouse" program on Sunday morning, where the basics of the Christian faith and spiritual growth are taught. Others attend our Wednesday night services or one of the adult congregations that meets on Sunday or at another time

during the week. Follow-up happens in many different ways, and we continue to add options for people who want to grow in the Lord.

Question 5: Do you advertise?

We advertise, but not in the traditional church ways. First, we have massive billboards posted at various places around the city; they display the "Saturday Night" logo and the time. Second, we advertise each week in the movie section of the daily newspaper and feature our logo and the topic for the week. Third, we run radio commercials on "easy listening," "light rock," and "oldies" stations in town. We do not advertise on Christian stations because most un-churched people do not tune into them. We try to develop commercials of genuine quality. Fourth, when college terms begin in the fall, we obtain permission to place a small flyer in all the students' mail boxes and in strategic places around town where students will see them. Fifth, and best, we rely on word-of-mouth.

Question 6: Do we have to use rock music?

In a word, no. But for us, the answer is yes. When we attempted to change the style of music, we met great opposition from the people who attend. Rock music connects with the people to whom we are ministering. It also allows us to break all notions of church tradition, which in our community is quite important. Many unchurched people have preconceived ideas about dead, formal, ortho-dox religion. When they enter our building and hear our band play, it is a clear reminder that this is not a traditional church setting. Each person will have to decide what is the most viable style of music for a seeker service. I believe that the style we use is the most appropriate for our purposes.

Question 7: Why do you dress in blue jeans?

We want people to feel completely comfortable when they attend "Saturday Night." A suit and tie imply a level of formality we do not want. So when people see me dressed in T-shirts, blue jeans, and running shoes, they know that however they are dressed, they fit in. Once in a while someone will show up in a suit, and he will look rather out of place. The informal look is in part an attempt to make people feel comfortable and to promote a congenial atmosphere.

Question 8: Why do you hold the seeker service in a church building? Why not move to a more neutral site?
We have thought a great deal about the location. In many ways it would be better to hold a Saturday night service in a more neutral setting, because we have to overcome the obstacle of a church auditorium. However, we concluded that we want people to become connected to the church eventually, so why not leap that hurdle right up front? I think that people gradually lose their hang-ups about walking into a church building. So we continue to hold the seeker service in a church building.

Question 9: Why don't you sing praise choruses?
During the first year we sang praise songs as part of the service. However, people did not respond and participate well. We concluded that unchurched people prefer to come and observe—not participate. We also felt that congregational singing had the feel of a more traditional church setting even though the band accompanied it. So we dropped the praise songs.

Question 10: Do many unchurched people attend?
We survey the congregation during the same month each year. One question we ask concerns previous church attendance. Our surveys indicate that about seventy percent of the people who attend "Saturday Night" do not attend church. Half of this seventy percent are church dropouts, and the other half have no church background at all.

Question 11: How much is your budget?
The budget varies from year to year, but has leveled off at about $50,000. The lion's share is spent on advertising—newspaper ads, billboards, and radio and television com-

mercials. The actual overhead for "Saturday Night" is quite low.

Question 12: Why do you collect an offering?
The comment that appears most frequently in our surveys is that we should stop passing an offering plate. Our analysis suggests that this comment comes primarily from Christians. No unchurched person has voiced an objection to passing the plate. We feel that at some point in one's connection to a church, the plate is going to be passed, and it might as well happen early on so that people do not think we have hidden agendas. We are careful how we talk about the offering; we tell people not to feel pressure to give, that the offering is primarily for those who attend regularly and want to help underwrite the expenses of "Saturday Night."

Question 13: Do the offerings cover the expenses?
The offerings average about one dollar per person. This covers about seventy percent of our budget. The rest is underwritten as an outreach of our church. We have discovered that the offerings have increased over the years as people become more connected and involved in "Saturday Night."

Question 14: Where do you get your drama scripts?
In the first two years we wrote all our dramas. Then we spent about a year and a half borrowing dramas from other sources, especially Willow Creek Community Church. This last year we have returned to writing most of the dramas ourselves. The drama people and I talk about ideas, then they create a script that generally represents the concept we want to communicate in a particular service.

Question 15: How did you form your band?
We were concerned at the outset about finding musicians, but an interesting thing happened. The musicians were sitting in the congregation on Sunday and looking for an opportunity to use their musical talents. Right now we have a surplus of musicians. People who play contemporary music have little opportunity to use their talents in a

traditional setting, and they are enthusiastic about being part of the band at "Saturday Night."

Question 16: Do the "Sunday people" support or criticize?
Sunday people do both. The vast majority are very supportive, and criticism arises only in regard to the music. However, even those who are critical of the music are at least tolerant enough to allow the program to happen and to appreciate what God is doing in people's lives. There are also more than 350 people who pray daily for "Saturday Night." Even though they do not attend, they feel connected to "Saturday Night" because they are the backbone of prayer for what we are doing.

Question 17: Does "Saturday Night" have any impact on what you do on Sunday?
"Saturday Night" has made me much more sensitive to people with little church background who may attend on Sunday. For example, in preaching, I invite people to use the Bibles that are in the pew racks. To help them find Scripture passages, I announce the page numbers. When we sing choruses or praise songs, the words are printed for people who do not know them by heart. These are some small ways in which "Saturday Night" has influenced Sunday services.

Question 18: Other churches have tried seeker-sensitive services and have failed. Why?
A major reason that churches fail is that they are not totally committed to the program. By commitment I mean the support and involvement of the senior pastor, the financial resources to ensure success, and the will to allow enough time for the program to happen.

Also, people observe what Willow Creek does and what we do and assume that all that they need is a good idea. They fail to recognize that underneath the Saturday night service is a strong structure of follow-up and of connecting people to the Lord and to each other.

Question 19: How do you develop topics?

We keep all the written questions on file. From time to time I sort through these and determine which are asked most often and thereby what is on people's minds. From this research we develop the topics. I also meet from time to time with a small group of people who have a high level of interest in "Saturday Night," and we explore potential topics together.

Question 20: Is it necessary to have an open question-and-answer session?

I believe that the Q and A is an important ingredient of "Saturday Night." It gives us an opportunity to respond to what is really on people's minds rather than assuming what they are thinking. When we first started the Q and A, we simply had people stand up and ask their questions orally. However, as the service grew, this became intimidating, and we discovered that people were more open with written questions.

Question 21: What is the future of "Saturday Night"?

I think the ultimate future of "Saturday Night" is essentially a separate congregation within our church. I am also aware that ten years from now, "Saturday Night" may be obsolete as a method for reaching people. We must constantly evaluate where we are, what we are doing, and whom we are reaching. We must be willing and open to changing "Saturday Night" when it is no longer effective.

Question 22: If you could start over, what would you change?

The first thing I would change is taking two months off during the summer. For the first four years we shut down the program for about eight weeks in summer, assuming that people would not attend. The fifth year, we kept the service going, and our attendance averaged 407 for the entire summer. By shutting down we were communicating to people that "Saturday Night" is not as important as what we do on Sunday.

Question 23: Were you influenced by Bill Hybels and Willow Creek Community Church?

I have met Bill Hybels and have been to services at Willow Creek, but I have not attended any of their pastor's conferences. In starting "Saturday Night" we were influenced indirectly by Bill Hybels. I had watched a video, had read some articles in the press, and had listened to some people from Calvary who had been at Willow Creek. But we did not set out to pattern our service after Willow Creek. We identified whom we wanted to reach and tried to build a service around the needs of those people. It happens that our service is similar to Willow Creek in some ways, but it is uniquely different as well.

Question 24: "Saturday Night" has not had the same explosive growth as the Sunday services. Why not?

In five years the Sunday attendance grew from 2,500 to nearly 5000. The "Saturday Night" attendance has grown to an average of a little more than 800 in 1993. I have wondered why Saturday does not explode like Sunday and have concluded that because many people who attend on Saturday night have a low level of commitment to the church and possibly no commitment to Christ, they do not feel a compelling need to come every week during the year. They attend if the topic interests them or if they are going through a personal struggle. Consequently, beyond a recognizable core of about 300, there are several hundred more who kind of float in and out. I think the long-term potential is for continued growth, but it will continue to be much slower than what we have experienced on Sunday.

Question 25: What is the single most critical factor in making "Saturday Night" happen?

Being committed to unchurched people is a high priority. If it is not a high priority, the ministry of the church will start with enthusiasm but ultimately fade away.

Question 26: How do you move from a program to a community?

Building community requires including people in service and ministry and instilling the desire for them to serve others. We do this through small-group Bible studies, support groups, one-on-one discipleship, and so on. From time to time I also mention publicly at "Saturday Night" people who need prayer and encourage the congregation to pray for them. As time goes by, we are becoming more and more a community and less and less a program.

Question 27: What are some of the dangers in designing a seeker service?
The first danger is to try to copy what another church does. It is damaging for people to imitate Willow Creek or Calvary Church or any other church. We can learn principles from others churches, but we have to apply those principles to our own situation in a culturally relevant way.

Question 28: Do you feel comfortable in this format of ministry?
It took me more than a year to begin feeling comfortable with this style of ministry. Many times I wondered whether I had compromised the faith and given up on much of my training and background. As I look back, I think that was a legitimate struggle. I am persuaded that we have neither compromised the faith nor given up on the Bible. Now I enjoy the format and really look forward to the seeker service every week.

Question 29: How do you respond to critics who say this is pure entertainment or slick marketing and you are giving people what they want, not what they need?
It is very difficult to respond to critics, because I have tended to become defensive and quote the Bible to them. But I have discovered that that approach has little impact. I believe there is nothing fundamentally flawed about entertainment or providing a setting that is culturally relevant in which people can hear the gospel. After all, many churches have padded pews, air conditioning, a good sound system, and other physical features that attempt to make people com-

fortable when they worship God. We must judge the ultimate intent and purpose of what we do. If our service is entertaining so that through the entertainment we can communicate the gospel and point people to Christ, then that is okay. Jesus told parables and stories—some of which were highly entertaining—to communicate truth. In the Old Testament, the prophets often illustrated truth through object lessons from their own lives.

Question 30: Why do you not give a public invitation?
In many evangelical churches it is assumed that the only way to call the unconverted to Christ is to give a public invitation and have people walk down an aisle. Salvation occurs when the Holy Spirit convicts people and brings them face to face with Jesus Christ. That *can* happen in walking down an aisle, but it happens elsewhere too. In our context, walking down an aisle puts people on the spot; it applies pressure that is inappropriate when people are fragile and confronted with their relationship to God. It can be manipulative. At the end of the "Saturday Night" talks, I usually ask a couple of people to stand up who will stay after the service to meet and talk and pray with visitors. I stay also. We find that this is much more effective than putting people on the spot. In fact, I seldom give a public invitation on Sunday for the same reason. On Sunday we provide a prayer room where people can find Christ.

EPILOGUE

This poem expresses well my desire to reach unchurched people. I discovered it in *A Guide to Prayer*, published by The Upper Room, Nashville, Tennessee. I read it often and find it encouraging and motivating each time.

I Stand by the Door
by Samuel Moor Shoemaker

I stand by the door.
I neither go too far in, nor stay too far out,
The door is the most important door in the world—
It is the door through which men walk when they find God.
There's no use my going way inside, and staying there,
When so many are still outside and they, as much as I,
Crave to know where the door is.
And all that many ever find
Is only the wall where a door ought to be.
They creep along the wall like blind men,
With outstretched, groping hands,
Feeling for a door, knowing there must be a door,
Yet they never find it . . .
So I stand by the door.

The most tremendous thing in the world
Is for men to find that door—the door to God.
The most important thing any man can do
Is to take hold of one of those blind, groping hands,
And put it on the latch—the latch that only clicks
And opens to the man's own touch.
Men die outside that door, as starving beggars die
On cold nights in cruel cities in the dead of winter—
Die for want of what is within their grasp.

They live, on the other side of it—live because they have
    not found it,
And open it, and walk in, and find him . . .
So I stand by the door.
Go in, great saints, go all the way in—
Go way down into the cavernous cellars,
Away up into the spacious attics—
It is a vast, roomy house, this house where God is.
Go into the deepest of hidden casements,
Of withdrawal, of silence, of sainthood.
Some must inhabit those inner rooms,
And know the depth and heights of God,
And call outside to the rest of us how wonderful it is.
Sometimes I take a deeper look in,
Sometimes venture in a little farther;
But my place seems closer to the opening . . .
So I stand by the door.

There is another reason why I stand there.
Some people get part way in and become afraid
Lest God and the zeal of his house devour them;
For God is so very great, and asks all of us.
And these people way inside only terrify them more.
Somebody must be by the door to tell them that they are
    spoiled
For the old life, they have seen too much:
Once taste God, and nothing but God will do any more.
Somebody must be watching for the frightened
Who seek to sneak out just where they came in,
To tell them how much better it is inside.

The people too far in do not see how near these are
To leaving—preoccupied with the wonder of it all.
Somebody must watch for those who have entered the door,
But would like to run away. So for them, too,
I stand by the door.
I admire the people who go way in.
But I wish they would not forget how it was
Before they got in. Then they would be able to help
The people who have not yet even found the door,
Or the people who want to run away again from God.
You can go in too deeply, and stay in too long,

And forget the people outside the door.
As for me, I shall take my old accustomed place,
Near enough to God to hear him, and know he is there,
But not so far from men as not to hear them,
And remember they are there, too.

Where? Outside the door—
Thousands of them, millions of them.
But—more important for me—
One of them, two of them, ten of them,
Whose hands I am intended to put on the latch.
So I shall stand by the door and wait
For those who seek it.
"I had rather be a door-keeper . . ."
So I stand by the door.

APPENDIX A

A SAMPLE SEEKER SERVICE

This appendix can at best capture only the essence of "Saturday Night." First, it is impossible to capture a visually oriented program in print. Second, it is impossible to capture the spirit of what people sing and say in writing.

Why did I choose this particular program? Because it was the program we did the week I was to prepare this appendix. At first I thought I would carefully select a program that is truly representative. But then I decided just to include what we did that week.

The following program was given on October 31, 1992—Halloween. We decided to relate the topic to satanism. Several weeks earlier, I met with Doug Fagerstrom, singles pastor and director of the drama department. I said my talk would focus on the temptations of Adam and Eve and Jesus. For a drama sketch, we came up with the idea of putting Adam and Eve in a modern setting.

We also proposed using the video about Satan performed by the Christian musician Carmen. But when we viewed the video we rejected it for two reasons: (1) the language is very theological and full of church jargon, and (2) it includes a statement about Satan cursing someone with AIDS. We felt that statement could be inappropriate and offensive to any HIV-positive people attending "Saturday Night."

The Opening

A seven-year-old dressed as a pirate walks down the middle aisle toward the platform. As he walks he says, "Trick or treat! Trick or treat!" When he reaches the platform he turns to the audience:

Hi, I'm Daniel and I'm looking for lots of candy. I don't see any here. So I'm going somewhere else. And by the way, welcome to "Saturday Night." Oh yes!

Immediately the band begins the introduction to the first song.

Wise Up
(Words and music by Wayne Kirkpatrick and Billy Simon)

Got myself in this situation
I'm not sure about
Climbing in where there's temptation
Can I get back out
I never can quite find the answer
The one I want to hear
The one that justifies my action
Says the coast is clear
Something on the outside
Says to jump on in
But something on the inside
Is telling me again

(Chorus)

Better wise up
Better think twice
Never leave room for compromise
You better wise up
Better get smart
And use your head to guard your heart
It's gonna get rough
So you better wise up

Take a look at your intentions
When you have to choose
Could it be that apprehension
Might be telling you
To back off now is better
So take your heart and run
But get your thoughts together
Before they come undone

(Repeat chorus)

To back off now is better
So take your heart and run
But get your thoughts together
Before they come undone

(Repeat chorus)

Welcome

After the song, I welcome the crowd:

Welcome to "Saturday Night." Tonight's topic is Satanism. At the end of the program tonight we will take time to respond to your questions about this topic. If you have a question or one comes to mind during the program, write it down. A place has been provided on the back of the program. Next week we begin a new series on the subject of prayer.

After the program tonight we have three options for those who would like to stay. First, we have "Singles Viewpoint." This is for singles, and the topic tonight is "Satanism and the Occult: A View of the Dark Side." We also have an Alcoholics Anonymous group and a Narcotics Anonymous group. All these groups meet downstairs. To get there, go to the back of the auditorium and down the stairwells in front of the green exit signs. We welcome you and hope you enjoy the rest of the program.

The band begins to play the theme from the movie *The Addams Family*.

The Drama
"The Addam's Family"
(written by Doug Fagerstrom)

CHARACTERS:

Adam	Dressed in solid-color sweats . . . a real slob
Eve	Dressed in solid-color sweats . . . a perfectionist
SG ("Some Guy")	Dressed in wild colors, flashy checked/plaid sports coat, briefcase . . . a real huckster

SETTING: A *messy* living room and kitchen table. Adam is sleeping on the couch. Eve is sitting in a chair.

VOICE: *(Organ background, churchlike)* So the Lord God caused the first man Adam to fall into a deep sleep; and while he was sleeping, he took one of the man's ribs. Then the Lord God made a woman from the rib he had taken and brought the woman to the man.

ADAM: *(Waking up with yawns, stretching and rubbing his side)* Oh, my aching side. I had the strangest dream last night. *(Keeps rubbing side)* Boy, this couch has got to go! My side is killing me! It must have been that pizza or those ribs I ate last night. *(Looks up)* Ah, God, I am trying to tell you, the single life is not for me. I sure wish you would listen to me. Now, where did I put the Pepto? *(Searching around, sees Eve, is startled)* Wow! Botta boom, botta bing! What are you?!

EVE: *(Coyly with some assertiveness)* I am a woman!

ADAM: *(Dumfounded)* Great! And what is a wo-man?

EVE: *(Exasperated)* Oh, brother! Why did I know this was going to happen? I guess I am just going to have to explain everything to you. *(Short pause)* Ah, are you any relation to the Flintstones? You remind me a lot of . . .

ADAM: By the way, what are you doing here? *(He leans over)* Did, ah . . . he *(Points up)* send you?

EVE: *(Flirtatiously)* And what do you think?

ADAM: I have been making a few requests about the single life and, well *(Looking her over)* . . . you do beat a rhino or one of those hippopotamuses.

EVE: *(Sarcastically)* That is the nicest compliment I have ever had. *(Under her breath)* It is the only one.

ADAM: Hey . . . cute stuff . . . are you into climbing trees?

EVE: Look, "big boy," I could do a lot for you!

ADAM: Yeah? Like what? *(Sits down on couch and begins to eat and starts "tuning out" into a newspaper)*

EVE: *(With a great air of confidence, taking charge)* First of all, I can teach you how to clean up after yourself. *(Picks up junk and looks rather disheartened)* Then again, I can teach you a lot about life. I think I can help you make a few better choices than the ones you have already made. For instance, I think we need to make a few changes. . . . Have you heard anything I have said? *(Doorbell rings)*

ADAM: *(Looks up from paper)* Sure, babe, haven't missed a beat . . . and you can begin by answering the door. *(Eve reluctantly, with a fist in her hand, moves to open the door)*

SG: Addam's Family? *(Eve responds)* Say, I was just passing through the neighborhood and thought I would see if I could be of some help to you and the hubby. I have a fine line of personal care and improvement products.

EVE: *(Desperately)* I am open to anything. You would not believe what I have to work with. Life for me is less than twelve hours old and I have been dealt a bad hand.

SG: *(Looking at Adam)* Hey, I think I know what you mean, but I can fix you up . . . no problem.

EVE: So, what do you have?

SG: First of all, I have a great line of Fuller Brushes. *(Shows a brush and booklet)*

EVE: I'll take them all!

SG: Great! Now, have you heard about . . . Amway? I think that you would make a great distributer and for only the small amount of . . .

EVE: *(Leans over to SG)* Will this Amway get me out of the house?

SG: Of course, you will have the . . .

EVE: Sign me up!

SG: Now, I think a few MaryKay Cosmetics would be right up your . . . *(Holds out a tube of lipstick)*

EVE: What are cosmetics?

SG: Make-Up! These little wonders will put magic into your man for those special moments when . . . *(Both start looking at Adam as he is sitting with his feet on the couch, reading the paper, and shoveling food into his mouth)* . . . the . . . two of . . . you . . . *(SG and Eve look at each other)*

EVE
and SG: Not!

SG: How about some cooking utensils? *(Holding a frying pan)*

EVE: *(Examines frying pan as a potential weapon)* No thanks!

SG: *(Picks an apple with a large price tag attached and holds it up admiringly)* Why, this the most wonderful, most powerful thing you have ever seen or heard of.

EVE: Will it slice and dice?

SG: It will change your life!

EVE: Yeah? How so?

SG: Lady, this will put you right at the top. You will be the envy of the neighborhood! Everyone will want what you have. Think of it! Power, fame, fortune, your name in lights—you can have it all!

EVE: *(She has not bought in yet)* How can I believe you?

SG: Hey, do I look like a . . . liar? Honesty is my business. "Big Guy" upstairs knows who I am. In fact, He is on my resume. He has called me a prince and an angel of light. Now, you don't see *Him* stopping me, do you? So, what could be so wrong? The choice is entirely yours!

EVE: *(Looks at large price tag on apple)* Oh, I don't know. It looks kind of expensive. In fact, this could cost a lot. *(Looks over to Adam)* Adam, what do you think?

ADAM: *(Responding with mouth full, looking over his newspaper)* Anything you say, babe! Checkbook is somewhere on the table. See if he'll take a postdated check.

SG: Hey, no problem! Our policy is get now and pay later . . . even if it is much later. Don't worry.

EVE: Okay, I'll take one. *(Showing some gratitude)* You know, I could not have done this without you. You have really helped me a lot. Besides, it's not like we are going to fall over dead or something! *(Responds with nervous laugh, SG leaves, Eve sits in chair staring at the apple)*

ADAM: Hey, Wo-man. Who was the little guy with the funny clothes?

EVE: *(Contemplatively)* I don't know. Just some nice guy— at least he wasn't pushy. *(Pause)* Adam, did you hear what he said about a new life, fame, fortune and all that other stuff?

ADAM: Sorry, babe, I wasn't paying much attention . . . it's not my job . . . I figure you can take care of the domestic stuff.

EVE: You just aren't going to be of any help, are you? *(Strong)* Well, I made a choice and I am going to stick with it, and I don't care what you say, even if you were the last man on earth. *(She cuts apple in half and puts it on his plate)*

ADAM: What a woman . . . she knows how to get to a guy's heart . . . through his . . . *(Stands, begins to rub stomach, then rubs side)* . . . boy, my side is killing me!

(Blackout)

Offering

I return to the stage to announce the offering. I say the following:

> This next part of the program is only for those who attend "Saturday Night" on a regular basis. It is our opportunity to give money to help underwrite the expenses of this program. We do not want anyone to feel pressure to give. This is only for those who want to give. Ushers please come forward.

The band plays a three-minute jazz/rock number while the plates are being passed.

Real Life

Phil Arena gives his testimony, which takes about five minutes. He walks to the platform and says,

Hi, my name is Philip and I want to tell you what Christ has done in my life. . . .

Song

Nothing Can Separate Us
(Words and music by James Isaac Elliot and Justin Peters)

In my moment of weakness
I don't know how I should pray
When I can't find the words
My spirit can be heard
Saying to me
Nothing can separate us,
There is no power below or above
Nothing can separate us
From His love

There is no condemnation
For Jesus is one Lord
He has set us free
From the law of sin and death
Eternally

Protector, Provider
All power is underneath our Lord's command
And always His voice says
We are His now
And for eternity

(Repeat chorus)

Scripture

Jesus, full of the Holy Spirit, returned from the Jordan and was led by the Spirit in the desert, where for forty days he was tempted by the devil. He ate nothing during those days, and at the end of them he was hungry.

The devil said to him, "If you are the Son of God, tell this stone to become bread."

Jesus answered, "It is written: 'Man does not live on bread alone.'" The devil led him up to a high place and showed him in an instant all the kingdoms of the world. And he said to him, "I will give you all their authority and splendor, for it has been given to me, and I can give it to anyone I want to. So if you worship me, it will all be yours."

Jesus answered, "It is written: 'Worship the Lord your God and serve him only.'"

The devil led him to Jerusalem and had him stand on the highest point of the temple. "If you are the Son of God," he said, "throw yourself down from here. For it is written:

"'He will command his angels concerning you to guard you carefully; they will lift you up in their hands, so that you will not strike your foot against a stone.'"

Jesus answered, "It says: 'Do not put the Lord your God to the test.'"

When the devil had finished all this tempting, he left him until an opportune time.

Talk

(The talk has not been edited to correct the grammar. It appears as it was given.)

Tonight I'm talking about the subject of Satan. Really, I'd like to pose several simple questions and then do my best to try to answer them. The first and most obvious questions is: Who is Satan? Most of us have an image of Satan. He's in a red aerobics workout suit, and he has a pitchfork. Other people think that there is no such a thing as Satan. That there is obvious evil and there is obviously bad things and obviously are dealing with drugs and crack and heroin and all of the rest of it—but Satan really doesn't exist as a person. Bad things exist, but not Satan.

It's interesting, if we take the Bible as the source to answer the question, several things become obvious about Satan. Number one, God created Satan. You're saying, "God created Satan? Then God is responsible for all sorts of evil?" Actually, Satan started out as a good angel. He was one of the beings that God created—angels that are in God's presence. In fact, Satan was one of the greatest angels of all. He was a beautiful creation, created by God. He had a special place of significance in heaven. But the day came when Satan decided that he had had enough of God. Kind of decided, "I have had enough!"

The Scripture records the fall of Satan. I'd like to paraphrase it and put it in my own language. Satan basically, one day, decided, "You know, I'm about as good as God. In fact, who needs God anyway? What I'd like to do is, I'd like to replace God." Essentially Satan said, "God, forget you, forget worshipping you, forget following you, forget submitting to you. I'm going to go out and make my own choice, do my own thing and be my own god." At that point, Satan was put out of heaven and turned from doing good, which is what he did when he was a good angel, to doing bad.

The two names for Satan, namely Satan and the Devil, tell us a lot about who Satan is. The word *Satan* means adversary or opponent. Purdue was almost a "Satan" to Michigan this afternoon. They almost pulled it off, but they didn't. It means an opponent. Someone who is against you. Someone that goes head to head. The word *Satan* tells us that Satan is an adversary, number one, of God and, number two, of each of us, desiring that we follow him rather than following God. The word *devil* means slanderer or deceiver or liar. I loved that drama a while ago. Doug, right down front, wrote the drama. I loved the line where the guy in the plaid pants and the plaid thing and the bright green coat—by the way, those garments are for sale afterwards for anyone who wants to make the latest statement in fashion in the greater Grand Rapids community. We would be happy to work out a deal. The guy says, "Do I look honest?" Satan is the slanderer. The word *devil* means a liar, deceiver, or a slanderer. So, who is Satan? He was created by God. He rebelled against God and he spends all of his time in opposition to God, in opposition to us and in lying and deceiving.

Question two, what is Satan like? He really has two sides—what I would call the dark side of Satan and what I would call the bright side of Satan. The dark side of Satan is getting a lot of attention these days. It deals with Satan worship.

I have a book with me tonight entitled *The Edge of Evil: The Rise of Satanism in North America* by a guy named Jerry Johnson, with a foreword by Geraldo Rivera. It's a whole book about the rising influence of Satanism in North America. The head of the prison—I believe it's in the state of Texas—having dealt with many Satanists in prison and having gotten connected all over the country with the problem of Satanism, estimated (and this is incredible) that every year between forty and sixty thousand human beings are killed in Satanic sacrifices worldwide. Now, living in Grand Rapids, that's beyond the stretch of my mind and imagination. But here's one of the leading experts in prisons and correction and Satanism and the occult saying that each year between forty and sixty thousand human beings are actually sacrificed.

The dark side of Satan is alive and well. It's communicated through much of the words of the dark side of heavy metal music. Groups like Slayer and Venom, Mega Death, Metalica. Not everything they do is satanic, but a lot of the message of the dark side of Satan is communicated through that kind of music. Obsession with death, with violence, with the occult, with the Satanic symbols, with Satanic worship. A lot of people dabble in it through fantasy games. For example, "Dungeons and Dragons" may appear on the surface to be a rather innocent game, but there is an increasing body of research that that can open the door to a pattern that ends up very self-destructive and destructive of others. Now, it doesn't always happen that way, but I think fantasy games, ouija boards, seances, the fact that the Satanic bible is one of the best-selling books in America—all of that combined opens up the door to the increasing influence of Satan worship. The dark side of Satan in North America.

But that's not what I want to talk about tonight because I want to talk about the light or the bright side of Satan. In the drama, Satan pulled out his resume and said, "The man upstairs calls me a prince and he calls me an angel of light." And that is true. The Bible calls Satan an angel of light. He doesn't always appear in darkness, in ritual, seances, and death and obsession with the dark side of human experience. Satan, I'm convinced, more often touches each of our lives on the bright side of life as an angel of light.

Think about the Creation story. Satan, who came as a serpent (the plaid dress was as close as we could get to a serpent tonight)—Satan came and his temptation was not "Dungeons and Dragons," it was not the occult, it was not Satan worship, it was not reciting the Lord's Prayer backwards, it was not imposing the satanic symbol on people. He said, "Here's a piece of fruit, eat it." I mean, what in the world could be so bad about a piece of fruit? What in the world could be so terrible about that? I'm convinced that the strategy of Satan impacts all of our lives tonight.

Having said that, I want to take a timeout to ask a question. As I begin to answer the question, you're going to immediately think, "What in the world does this have to do with Satan?" And when I work my way through it, at the end of it, hopefully I'll be able to demonstrate how directly this is connected to Satan.

The question is this: Bottom line, what is life all about? That's a pretty important question. What in the world is the meaning and purpose of life? I'd like to suggest that in answering the question, what is life all about? there are at least three options, three choices.

Number one, life is what I experience. You could put in parenthesis "self-satisfaction." That meaning is not found in other people. Meaning is not found in religion. Meaning is not found in Christ. Meaning is not found in the church. The ultimate purpose and meaning of life is being satisfied, having a good time, enjoying life. So what is life? What I experience.

Number two. What is life? Second option: What I get. Here we're thinking about he who has the most toys wins. We're familiar with that kind of philosophy. Life—you only go through it once. Some people say, "It's being satisfied, it's finding happiness, it's finding fulfillment." Often that can lead to drugs and a lot of bad and destructive things, but some people think that life is what I get. And that you measure my life by the cars I drive, the clothes I wear, the job I have, the income I have, and all of the toys and the watches and everything else that I possess.

The third option, which is a little more sophisticated is, life is not what I experience or what I accumulate, life is what I know. Here in America this is a big one. That what's important in life is knowledge. Getting the right degree. Going to the right school. Studying the right major in order to get the right job so you can accumulate the right things so that ultimately you can be satisfied. While satisfaction and things are important, the only way you get either is by getting knowledge. Who am I? I am a graduate of whatever school. Who am I? This is what I know. Who am I over here? Look at me, the clothes I wear, the cars I drive, the things I accumulate. Who am I? I'm a satisfied person living life.

I want you to think about these three options because these are precisely the temptations of Satan. First of all to Adam and then to Jesus Christ. In fact, there's a Bible in the rack in front of you. It's the smaller of two books. If you would turn to the first book of the Bible—that's the book of Genesis. The word *genesis* means beginning. This will be page number three. You'll see two columns and if you'll come down to the bottom of the first column there is a big number three. Above that it says, "The Fall of Man." Here's how it's described—not quite the way it was portrayed tonight, but pretty close.

> Now the serpent [that's referring to Satan] was more crafty [that means he's a deceiver, manipulative] than any of the wild animals the LORD God had made. He said to the woman [this is Eve], "Did God really say, 'You must not eat from any tree in the garden'?"

The first thing Satan does is try to discredit what God said.

> The woman said to the serpent, "We may eat fruit from the trees in the garden, but God did say, 'You must not eat fruit from the tree that is in the middle of the garden, and you must not touch it, or you will die.'"

Satan answers,

> "You will not surely die," the serpent said to the woman. "For God knows that when you eat of it your eyes will be opened, and you will be like God, knowing good and evil."

Now watch carefully.

> When the woman saw that the fruit of the tree was good for food [for self-satisfaction it looked like it was good to eat] and pleasing to the eye,

She observed it as a thing. This is some*thing* that I would like to have.

> and also desirable for gaining wisdom [for getting knowledge],

When she saw that it would satisfy her, that it was pleasing, that it was a thing that she could possess and when she was aware that this would increase her knowledge,

> she took some and ate it.

Now turn over to the New Testament. It's the gospel of St. Matthew and it's on page number 1009. This is where Satan comes to Jesus Christ. He does not tempt him into occult worship, into repeating the Lord's Prayer backwards or any other thing like that. Second column by the big number four.

> Then Jesus was led by the Spirit into the desert to be tempted by the devil. After fasting forty days and forty nights, he was hungry. The tempter came to him and said, "If you are the Son of God, tell these stones to become bread."

Jesus is hungry. He has a physical need. He needs physical satisfaction. Satan comes and says, "Here's some rocks. Why don't you turn them into bread?" Now if I were able to cook or bake, I could do the reverse—I could turn bread into stones in my baking process. But Satan says, "Take these rocks, make them bread. You have a need—a need to be satisfied. Why don't you go ahead and perform a miracle and take care of your need?" And Jesus responds.

Come down to the verse five. There's a little number five in the column.

> Then the devil took him to the holy city and had him stand on the highest point of the temple. "If you are the Son of God," he said, "throw yourself down. For it is written: 'He will command his angels concerning you, and they will lift you up in their hands, so that you will not strike your foot against a stone.'"

Satan now comes and tempts Jesus with knowledge. Satan starts quoting the Bible. He says, "Aren't you aware that because you are the Son of God, if you jump off this thing, God will take care of you? You'll not get hurt." So he is tempted to exercise knowledge. And Jesus resists.

Then the third thing. Turn the page to page 1010. The devil took him to a high mountain, showed him all the kingdoms of the world and their splendor. "All of this, all of these things, I'll give you if you will bow down and worship me." He showed Jesus all of the kingdoms and the power and glory of the world and said, "I'll give you all of this stuff, if you'll fall down and worship me."

Here's the strategy of Satan. It's a continuum that looks like this: Do we have needs, things that we need in our lives? Yes, we have to eat, we have to drink. There are certain things that all of us need for existence. But the temptation of Satan is to take these to an extreme where we pursue experiences and pleasure and ignore God—not realizing that our greatest need in life is to experience God in a personal relationship. What does Satan want to do? He wants to get us going in this direction where we pursue self-satisfaction, pleasure, whatever and in the process ignore God. Are there certain things that we need? Yes, we need clothes, we need shelter, we need jobs. Those are all things that we need, but the strategy of Satan is to cause us to pursue all of these things and ignore the most important thing in all of our life. And that is to have a personal relationship with God.

Do we need knowledge? Absolutely. A lot of people sitting here tonight have been to college and beyond. Yes, there are things that we need to know, but Satan wants us to pursue knowledge and ignore God. Not realizing that the most important thing that we can know is that we are rightly related to God. That's the bright side of Satan. That's not satanic symbols, not satanic sacrifice, that's not all of the bad dark stuff that you normally think about when you think of Satan. But these are areas where Satan makes inroads in the lives of human beings by saying, "Go after it and ignore God." Accumulate things. The more stuff you accumulate, the more important you are and ignore God. Knowledge—so important. Western culture—we worship at the shrine, at the ivory tower, of knowledge. Satan's strategy is to get us as human beings to pursue these and ignore the most important experience, the most important thing, and the most important knowledge, which is God.

I'd like you to think briefly tonight about how God looks at this world. Anybody full-blooded Irish here tonight? Or Irish ancestry or roots? You're half-Irish. That's good, Sean! How many (I hate to ask it) are Dutch? Good grief! Overwhelming! I thought I heard a lot of wooden shoes on the way in. What other nationalities or ethnic backgrounds are represented here tonight? German—French—African. How many out of African roots? Good number. What else do we have? Greek. How many Greek? Several people. What else do we have here tonight? Hungarian—Scandinavian—Scottish (that's good)—Lithuanian—English—Indian (India Indian).

Now, the world in which we live is filled with different countries, different backgrounds, different cultures. But as God looks down on the world, he really only sees two countries and two kings. The one king is Satan who rules over his country, and the other king is God who rules over his country. We've already identified that Satan is the enemy of God—the liar, the deceiver, the slanderer. That Satan's strategy is to get us as human beings to pursue pleasure, to pursue things, to pursue knowledge, and to ignore God.

Now, the bad news is that as human beings this is where we live. We are born slanted in Satan's direction. That doesn't mean that everybody is a Satanist, that everybody goes out and worships Satan. It simply means that the direction of my life is to choose "me" and to ignore God. So the question then is, If we are over here, how do we emigrate? How do we take up citizenship papers and get out of Satan's influence and into God's kingdom. The answer is, the cross of Jesus Christ. There is only one way.

Philip talked about it tonight. Many people who come here— you know what he was talking about—the awful addiction to drugs that destroyed his life. George is sitting back here, who will lead the AA group. He's sitting in a nice sweater, he's a businessman, but his story is just like Philip's. Not the streets of New York City, not crack houses, George has talked about how alcohol destroyed his life. It can be very obvious or not so obvious. Any attempt to live my life apart from God is giving in to the strategy of Satan.

The good news is that there is a way out. There is freedom. There is liberation. And it comes through Jesus Christ, who came into this world, who took our sin on himself, who died and who rose again so that through Christ we can move out of Satan's kingdom into what the Bible calls the kingdom of God.

Q and A
(Unedited)

1. *TV, newspapers, and the media consider Halloween a holiday. Doesn't a "holiday" come from "Holy Day"? If so, shouldn't Christians try to change this wrong?*

There is a lot of controversy over this issue of Halloween. And I'm not sure I know all of the background in regard to Halloween as a holiday. I do know that it's one of the satanic high days. But so is December 24. So if we can't do any celebrating or anything special on Halloween, then we probably shouldn't do any Christmas Eve programs on December 24th either. I think the greater question is, What does it mean to you and what does it mean for you to celebrate that?

I personally—and this is just my personal opinion—I don't see anything wrong with trick-or-treat. My understanding is, a lot of that is rooted in Irish folklore and dealing with the spirits—which is all news to me, even though I grew up in Ireland. When we came to the states and went trick-or-treating on Halloween, I'd never heard of that. I think it all depends on the situation and circumstances and how you celebrate it and what your intent is in doing it. I do get a little concerned with all the witches and so forth that's associated with Halloween, because that tends to minimize that as something just kind of cute and cartoon-like. If I understand the Bible correct, there is really not much cute about Satan and his power and influence.

2. *Should you let your children dress up as witches, goblins?*

I personally would have difficulty with that. That was my little boy who was dressed up tonight and came down the aisle. He was supposed to be—was it Red Beard, Captain Hook's assistant in the movie *Hook?* Is that who it is? He has all his lines down. I was trying to talk him into giving some of those lines tonight, but he said he would have to have the music from *Hook* to be able to do that. So I don't think I would want him dressed up as a witch or something directly associated with Satan.

3. *What is Satan's role in the world today?*

I think he has a multiple role. The Scriptures indicate, first of all, that he is the adversary of God. So his first role is to oppose God's plan and God's purposes in the world. He can do that on an individual level. I think he can do that on an institutional level. I do think he can also influence governments and whole cultures and thereby control people.

I don't know if you've ever been to Haiti, but I have visited all over the island of Haiti. When Haiti gained its freedom, the leaders of the country officially dedicated Haiti to Satan. I don't know if you're aware of that. But Haiti is the only country in the world that was officially dedicated to Satan. If you know anything about life in Haiti, there is a lot of satanic-related voodoo and witchcraft. I remember going to sleep at night to the sound of the witch doctor's drums up in the hills—which was a real reminder to me that the stuff about Satan is real.

Then I think, secondly, Satan tries to distract us as Christians. Maybe not directly, but indirectly from doing what the Lord would want in our lives.

4. *I have knowledge that my sister was actively unfaithful in her marriage. I have prayed for her and do and encouraged her and her husband to get counseling. They won't go. Is there more that I can do?*

One thing I think we all have to come to terms with is that you can't change another person's behavior. We tend to think that we can. But you really can't make somebody else do something that they don't want to do. Philip can come and talk about this. When he was all messed up on drugs, you could go talk to him all you want till you were blue in the face, but he had to make the choice of saying "yes" to Christ and saying "no" to drugs. So first of all, you have to understand that you can pray, you can encourage, but you can't make somebody else do what's right. I would simply encourage you to keep praying and keeping the relationship open so that they will talk to you.

5. *Is it right for Christians to participate in Halloween activities like costume dressing, trick-or-treating?*

I really didn't come prepared to answer those questions. I think it all depends on the individual. For me, I have made the choice that I will let my kids go trick-or-treating. I have very good Christian friends who wouldn't dare let their kids go trick-or-treating because they are absolutely against it. I respect their conviction, and I would hope that they would respect mine, because I don't believe that I'm promoting Satan or affirming Satan. In fact, it gives me an opportunity to talk to my kids about how people have taken this and how bad things do happen on Halloween and that Satan is therefore alive and well.

6. *Why is Halloween never spoken about in churches today? People should be made aware of its evilness.*

Again, I think evil depends on how you perceive it. Maybe I'm blind and maybe I'm ignorant and maybe I don't know all of the information I should know, but to me what makes something evil is your personal intent in regard to it.

7. *If Satan is not allowed to touch me unless God says so, why would God ever let him tempt me? Is it a test in my faith in God?*

I do believe that Satan can tempt people. I mean, we read that he tempted Jesus. I seriously doubt if Satan has ever tempted me. I'm serious. My problem is really not Satan. My problem is my own flesh, my own desires, my own heart. The reason I don't think Satan has ever tempted me—maybe he has, but I doubt that he has—is because I struggle enough with my own humanness and my own desire at times to do what is wrong. I think that is part of the struggle. Don't let anybody ever tell you if you become a Christian that all your problems will go away and you'll never make a bad choice. Wrong! Absolutely wrong! What God promises is to give you strength to face those choices individually. I think God allows Satan time on earth to do his work, knowing ultimately that he (God) will triumph.

8. *My family insists that God did not create Satan, evil, or sin. I disagree. They also believe that God predestined each of our lives so nothing happens by chance. What are your thoughts on this? Does this make sense? What does the Bible say? Is God the author of sin?*

God, number one, is not the author of sin, the source of sin. God created angels and human beings as a reflection of himself. One of the ways in which we reflect God is our ability to make choices and to create things. Because God makes choices and God created the world. So God created human beings with the ability to make choices; he did not create us as automated robots that simply responded to the buttons he pushed. God created Adam and Eve, as you saw tonight, with the ability to make choices.

God set some boundaries. Those boundaries, frankly, sound rather foolish. "Don't eat the fruit of the tree." That's really kind of a stupid rule. But nevertheless, that was the guideline. The reason for that was to allow human beings to make a choice. Will I follow God from my heart, or will I do my own thing? And you know the story from the Bible: Adam and Eve did their own thing. God created human beings with the ability to make choices. We are responsible for the choices, then, that we make—just as Satan was responsible for the choice that he made.

The question about predestination. That's a complicated term which means that God determines ahead of time everything that happens in a person's life. I happen not to believe that. I believe that God has established broad boundaries in which we live and in which we make choices. If we choose to overstep those boundaries, we suffer the consequences of those choices. I don't believe, for example, if I fall off the platform tonight that God way ahead of time determined that I—Saturday, Halloween—I would fall off the platform. I believe if I fall off the platform it's because I'm clumsy and not watching where I'm going. Or the clutter of this junk up here—some of you walked in tonight and looked up and said, "They brought my apartment up here tonight. Where did they get all this stuff?" I think God operates within broad principles and broad boundaries in our lives.

8. *Until about three years ago I was a member of the Satanic Church and a priest. I gave my life to Christ when I saw one of my best friends die because of that church. How will I know that the Lord has forgiven me?*

See right here? That's the cross. The only way I know God has forgiven me is that he demonstrated his love and he demonstrated his forgiveness by sending his Son into the world. God also promised that he would forgive me through Jesus Christ. I would encourage you to memorize some of God's promises in regard to forgiveness, such as—

> If we confess our sins, he is faithful and just and will forgive us our sins and purify us from all unrighteousness. First John 1:9.

Closing Prayer

After the questions, I explain the optional sessions meeting downstairs and the topic for next week. Then I ask people to stand for a closing prayer.

APPENDIX B

Q & A

These questions and answers all come from a four-week series called "Starting Over." It is hoped that the answers communicate a spirit of sensitivity and encouragement. The answers are slightly edited. Quotations from Scripture are paraphrases.

Starting Over . . .
How Can I After a Broken Relationship?
4 January 1992

1. *If I know the person I was dating was not the right person for me, how do I move into other relationships? I have accepted, I have forgiven, but I still love. Help me!*

First of all, love—that is a broad term because we use it in different ways. For example, I can say I love my wife, I love my children, and I love Notre Dame. But obviously those are different expressions of the same thing. We tend to think of love primarily in terms of emotions, but according to the Scriptures, love has at least three dimensions. First, love is emotional. Second, love is physical. Third, love is spiritual—which involves making the right decisions.

It appears that you have made a correct spiritual decision: "This person is not for me; better now to break off the relationship than continue that relationship and be deeply disappointed and hurt down the road." However, your emotions and feelings have not caught up with that choice yet. That's okay. Eventually I will work through them. Eventually I will be able to find a relationship that is correct and proper, in which love in all three dimensions can be expressed—spiritually, emotionally, and physically.

2. *How do you help a victim of sexual abuse or people who are hurting terribly?*

134

First of all, by loving them. Second, by not abusing them. Third, by encouraging them to seek professional help. I am convinced as I talk with victims of sexual abuse and with therapists that it is very important to seek professional help. Abusive situations tend to affect future relationships. We often pass that abuse or that abusive pattern on to people later on. So if you know a victim, love her for who she is, not what she can do.

Do not abuse the victim because she is vulnerable and fragile.

Encourage the victim to get help. Recovery does not come quickly. Insensitive people may say, "Get over it," or "It's no big deal." It *is* a big deal. It is an incredibly big deal, and people need time and help to work through that.

3. *Where is the joy in all this pain?*

I do not think there is any joy in pain. That idea is kind of masochistic in the sense that we can go around pumped up about pain. I have known a few football players of the "no-pain-no-gain" mind-set, but real life is not like that. The Bible tells us in the book of James, "Count it all joy when you encounter various trials." How in the world can we have joy in midst of trial? The joy that the Bible speaks of is not an outward happiness, but an inner strength that says, "I don't like this, and it is not pleasant and it sure hurts a lot, but I know that God is able to see me through. And I know, as Bonnie shared tonight, that God will teach me through this process, that I will become a better person, that I will be drawn closer to God as a result." In that sense there is an inner joy, an inner peace, in knowing that God will see me through.

4. *What if I don't have any depression? Is that denial?*

I cannot generalize, because everyone's circumstances and experiences are different. For some, the toughest part may be the denial stage. For others, it may be the depression stage. Not everybody goes through a struggle the same way, but these things do affect us. Some people are able to work through pain quicker than others for a variety of reasons. The key is, have I worked through it to the point of accepting it and going on?

5. *When I pray, why doesn't God make the pain go away? I know I have to be patient.*

Why doesn't God make the pain go away? I cannot answer except to say that one of the realities of our human existence is pain. No one is immune from pain. We all experience it. God never promised in the Scriptures to make pain go away; he only promised that in our pain he would be with us. He would give us strength. The Scriptures put it this way: "Count it joy when you fall into different kinds of trouble, knowing that the testing of your faith produces patience." The word *patience* means living under adversity. When God allows pain in our lives or when we experience pain, first, it is God's way of getting our attention, and second, it is precisely at that point that God will enter in and give us the strength to live underneath that pain.

6. *How can we be careful about whose help to accept without missing the help altogether?*

Recall Bonnie's testimony tonight. If you are going through what she has gone through or something similar, you may have to get help outside your family, your friends, or a minister. That is not an embarrassing thing to do. It does not mean you are weak or incapable of facing those problems. It simply means that you need a coach to call "time out" so you can step away from the emotion of the game that you're in and gain some sense of strategy and some plays to run to see it through so you make it to the final buzzer. I encourage you always, when you are going through deep struggles, to reach out to people, particularly Christian counselors who can help you work through them.

Starting Over . . .
How Can I After Great Personal Loss?

11 January 1992

1. *Forgiveness does not require or guarantee a change in the actions of the person forgiven. Therefore, how should a Christian act after forgiving someone if that person is likely to hurt you again?*

If at all possible, do not put yourself in a situation where you will get hurt again. Sometimes that is not possible. If, for example, the hurt lies in a marriage relationship, then your act of forgiveness should lead to the next step in the process, which is working with your spouse toward a healthy relationship and, if necessary, seeking some outside help to achieve that.

2. *What do you do when the person who hurts you wants to reconcile and you agree, but you find out they are continually lying to you and they admit it?*

Every good relationship—and this according to the Scripture—is built on a series of fundamental principles. Among those principles is honesty. The Bible says "Stop lying, start telling the truth. Speak the truth in love." Honesty and truthfulness are essential ingredients in building a healthy relationship. If you are working through the factors that contributed to a broken relationship and there is still dishonesty or lying going in, let me give you a big word of caution before you jump back in. You need to work through the root causes of that dishonesty and lying. Otherwise you will end up in a very unhealthy and, I might add, nonscriptural relationship that is not based on the principle of honesty.

3. *Sometimes it seems very difficult for an interested person to fit into the attitude of the Christian church. How does an introvert get in? Can an introvert be a Spirit-filled believer?*

We all have different personalities. Some people are very quiet, restrained, and shy; others are not. The two guys who sat out here on the couch in the drama for tonight's service are not introverts. They do the openings for "Saturday Night" quite regularly, and they ponder some basic ideas before they walk out and then go with whatever comes up. Sometimes what happens is wonderful and sometimes it is not. It was great tonight. So being introverted is not their problem.

For someone who is naturally introverted, the key to becoming involved in any group, including the church, is to lock into a smaller group of people, where you can feel a level of comfort. For example, if you are shy or reserved, get involved with something like a Bible study tomorrow night or some of the other small-group activities that go on here or wherever you go to church. I think getting involved is a little easier in a smaller group setting. Then you can get connected. Then you can begin building trust.

4. *If a person does something terrible to you and you forgive them and they know they are wrong but don't wish to come to you and apologize, how does God feel about that person?*

I suspect you want me to say God will zap that person for a lack of repentance and concern. But I won't say that because if that were the case, God would probably zap all of us—none of us quite live up to the right kinds of expectations. Forgiveness is something that *I* do. I can't make somebody else forgive me. I can encourage him to forgive me. I can be honest with her about the need of forgiveness, but we can't make another person forgive us. So I forgive, not to make the other person forgive me, but because it is the right thing for me to do.

What about the other person? He or she will continue to live chained to the wall until circumstances or people or God brings him or her to the point of being willing to forgive. We can't make that person forgive. In all of the injustices of life—and there are many—I am thankful (and I don't think this is a religious, anti-intellectual copout) that ultimately God keeps the record. And it is our hope that God can be trusted even though very difficult and painful things happen.

5. *My boss is determined to tell me that the Bible is not credible. I feel it is my responsibility and opportunity to witness to him, so how do I tell him the Bible is infallible and witness to him?*

Just argue with him and yell at him—no, no, no. An interesting verse in the Bible—it's from the writings of Paul, and Paul wrote most of the New Testament. Paul is writing to a group of people and says this: "You are our letters, you're my letter, not written with ink, not written on parchment, but you are the letter that I have written."

You say, "What does that have to do with my boss?" Option number one is to argue and defend the Bible. Option number two is to live out the Bible and let your life be the letter that he sees, that he reads, that he interacts with. Sometimes we forget that our lives are letters. We want to cram the Bible down someone's throat when maybe the greater opportunity and witness to the Christian is the letter that God is writing in our lives as others look at us. I read in the Bible that when the people saw the confidence and boldness and courage of the early disciples, they were amazed and took an interest in them and concluded, "Those people have been with Jesus." So I encourage you to live out the letter of the Bible in your life, and your living that out will open up opportunities to witness from the Scriptures.

6. *Do I trust again after my ex-wife cheated on me and now seems to be led by Satan?*

Trusting again is not an option like electric windows in an automobile or like turning on the radio. After trust has been violated, you don't say, "Okay, I've been hurt. Let me switch the button over and let me trust again." You have to work through a process. Yes, trust can be restored. But to restore that trust takes time and prayer and struggle and effort, and sometimes when you have been deeply wounded, it takes the help of a Christian counselor or a professional to help you work through that.

7. *It hurts so bad. Extremely hard to forgive. I'm in the thirty-year-old category. How can I possibly teach my seven-year-old and three-year-old how to forgive and let go of the past? Daddy left us.*

I am not sure how to respond to this. I believe your children will probably respond to that pain in a way similar to the way you have responded to it. I encourage you to work through some of the things we have talked about tonight. Work through the process. Learn to forgive, to let go, release that person. As your children see you doing that, they will then begin to live that out as well.

I wish that, as we heard earlier tonight, we could wave a wand and say there will not be more divorce and that every dad would love his children and every mom would love her children and every husband would be committed to his wife and every wife committed to her husband. The pain of broken family relationships is incredible. But I hold out the hope that God made a promise that he would be a father to the orphans, that he takes a special interest in broken families and broken relationships.

That may sound trite and simplistic, but I just encourage you to work through the process in your own life and get the help of others or get into a support group and tune in to God. If you have never trusted Christ, I hope you will receive him and build your relationship and your home as a single parent on the Scriptures. And God will help you through and so will people who love you. And so ought the church. The church has a great obligation to hurting families.

Starting Over . . .
How Can I After All My Failures?

18 January 1992

1. *How can God love me when I always seem to do the wrong thing and I dislike myself so much? I feel as if my life is a failure. I'm committed to the Lord, but I feel as if I fail him.*

You have expressed what probably many people in this room feel, me included. How can God love us when we seem to fail him repeatedly? He loves us because it is precisely what God specializes in doing. Our understanding of love is basically conditional. I love you—if you don't embarrass me, we say to our kids. I love you—if you don't throw the fried eggs in the restaurant this morning. I love you—if you do A, B, C, and D. So love has a lot of conditions. But God does not love with conditions. God loves us, and the truth is, whether I do good or bad, God loves me the same.

Remember that as persons we have significant value. Many people struggle with this because we tend to base our value on how we look or where we went to college or our ability to perform or our vocation. I am not quite as valuable as this other person because I can't do the kinds of things he or she can. The truth is that every human being is valuable and has significant worth for two reasons. First, we were created by God and that automatically gives us inherent value. Second, we were loved by God, and Jesus Christ came into the world, died on the cross, and shed his blood, and rose again so that we can experience a relationship with God. I have value because I am created by God and because God sent his only Son to restore me to a relationship with him. Be encouraged in that though all of us fail, God still loves us.

2. *After making a wrong choice in my life, I've been working on getting back to a more healthy way of life. I know God has a plan for me, but I have such a hard time giving up all my control of my life and having trust in his plan. Do you have any helpful advice for me? I am very frustrated with myself, knowing how happy I could be to have faith and trust in God.*

Yielding to God or having faith in God—people throw around a lot of theological terms that on the surface seem very confusing—accepting God or trusting God or believing in God: All these terms incorporate the same thing, which is the recognition that God has a claim on me and that God ought to have first place in my life.

The problem is that often our ability to trust God is damaged by people we have trusted who have hurt us. This often happens in a family as we grow up. I am reminded of Suzanne Sommer's book *Keeping Secrets*. If you have experienced an abusive home situation—for example, where your Dad abused alcohol and got violent and cussed you and called you all sorts of filthy names—those things are etched in your memory and you can't seem to erase them, so it is very hard to turn to God and understand him in the terms of a father. Sometimes what is needed is to work through the hurts and pains of previous relationships to learn to forgive, to let go, to get beyond that pain before you can begin to trust God in a healthy way. Working through the pain is one way to reach the point of having faith in God.

There is a second way. The Scriptures say that faith—trusting God—comes from hearing the Scriptures. We can increase or encourage our faith by spending time reading the Scriptures, and I encourage you to do this.

3. *I have made some crucial choices in the past three months. Those choices have changed my life for the better. I am living a more healthy life, but it's hard to maintain my health. I'm in college. How can I keep from getting depressed when I say no to friends and to temptations that I know would be a threat to my health and make me fall back into my bad habits?*

Two thoughts come to mind. One is the last line of the movie *Hook*: "Life is an adventure." It is a great line. "Life is an adventure"—but I want to add the phrase "one day at a time." If you are struggling with past choices that have hurt you and now you have resolved to go straight, to do right, to make good choices, don't make the commitment to do it till the day you die. Don't swear, "I'll never do it again." Jesus said, "Sufficient for every day is the evil you face." The Christian life—accepting Christ and wanting to live for him—is lived, not a year at a time, but one day at a time— or even, in some cases, one hour at a time or one moment at a time. Every day ask God to give you the help and strength to get through that day.

My second thought is, as the Bible puts it, "We are to bear each other's burdens and so fulfill the law that Jesus has given us." The law is, you shall love your neighbor as yourself. Build around you people who are making the same healthy choices you are, to become a support network so that when you are at rock bottom and you are ready to cave in, you can call somebody or go see somebody who will pray with you, encourage you, and affirm you.

4. *As a new Christian I have a hard time forgiving myself for things and it's hard to believe that God would forgive me. I can't forgive myself.*

I encourage you to get a Bible, if you don't have one—a Bible with an index in the back—and look up the word *forgiveness* and check all the references to forgiveness that are listed in the Bible. We must understand how God has forgiven us and has put all our sin behind us, never to be brought up again. One day when I stand before God, God will not say, "Dobson, let me punch that in the computer. Oh, my goodness! The printout is incredible! Do you remember on such-and-such a day at such-and-such a time, such-and such . . .?" No! God has an erase button. Have you ever wished you could hit an erase button after you have done something miserable? God has an erase button that covers our lives, and he will never play that tape again. The problem is, our minds don't have that erase button. Forgiveness, letting go of the past, is both an act (something you do at a specific time) and a process (because invariably it comes up again). Any of us can tell you the times when our wrongs come to mind—"Why in the world did I do that? I wish I could go back and make a better choice." When those feelings return, you forgive again, you let go again. You say, "Lord, I know you have forgiven me, and I know you are not going to bring it up, so I release myself again. Give me the strength to get through today."

5. *What advice would you offer to a sincere Christian who has tried many, many times to stop an alcoholic problem, but keeps failing.*

My first advice is to look in the Yellow Pages under Alcoholics Anonymous and start attending AA meetings. One AA group meets here at Calvary on Tuesday nights. Many of the people who attend AA here are committed Christians. You need that kind of support group to help you sort out your situation.

Starting Over . . .
Can God Give Me a Second Chance?
25 January 1992

1. *You say God separates our sin from us as far as the east is from the west. Does he continue to do that throughout our Christian experience, or does sin become an issue as far as losing our salvation? What about intentional sin?*

The idea that God removes our sin from us relates to the penalty or the consequences of our sin. The result of sin is separation from God. When I accept Christ and ask his forgiveness, he takes that penalty away and gives me eternal life. This does not mean that at that moment I become perfect, I still make choices. I still may do things that displease God, and when I do, it is my responsibility to confess that sin. I believe that when we commit our lives to Christ, it is as Jesus said: "I give unto them eternal life." That simply means life that will never end.

2. How do you start over when everyone else around you is still drinking and living the life that you want to get away from; that you want to start over and get straightened out?

The book of Psalms says that "blessed is the person who does not walk in the wisdom of ungodly people or stand in the way of sinners or sit in the seat of mockers." What that means is, if I struggle with detrimental things in my life, I had better be very careful about associating with people who are doing those things. Getting straightened out means, first, getting reconciled in your relationship to God. Second, it is important to build into your life positive peer influence. If you have a drinking problem, get involved in AA. Get around some other people who will encourage you. The Bible talks about it this way: "Provoke one another to love and good deeds." You need to be around people who are constantly stirring you and motivating you to do good deeds. Sometimes getting straightened out involves making a complete break with the friends who are drinking or doing drugs or living the kind of lifestyle that you are trying to break away from.

3. Where was the perfect God when, as a 3, 4, 5, 6, 7, 8, 9, and 10-year-old, I was sexually and emotionally abused? It's one thing if God can give me a second chance, but can I give God a second chance?

I have no simple answer. I don't know where God was. I know he is there now. I know that whatever we go through, he can bring healing to our lives. The only consolation I can offer to people who have really struggled is that God sent his Son to be completely abused by people who hated him, and God didn't have to do that. That incredible demonstration of God's love somehow gives hope in a very messed-up and terrible world. I think you can give God a second chance, but it entails a high risk. He can demonstrate healing and grace and hope and significance in your life in spite of all the things you were robbed of in your childhood. Frankly, in situations like this I almost wish God were Terminator III, to blow away people who have been so abusive and so hurtful. But the incredible thing about God is his love and his forgiveness. He can and does make a difference in your life. I encourage you to try to give God a second chance and to determine out of that terrible experience how you can reach out to other hurting people and help them.

4. What if we fall into sin over and over again?

The Scriptures tell us that with every temptation to sin, God has made a way to escape. I encourage you, whatever your personal struggle to sort out what the escape mechanism is for you in that particular temptation.

5. *Will God forgive me if I refuse to let go of my "book"—as in the skit, I use them to keep me in place.* (The "book" is a reference to the drama, in which a person kept writing down all her rejections and failures.)

First, when you ask God for forgiveness, God removes your sin as far as the east is from the west. Second, accept that forgiveness and be willing to let go of your past. Sometimes it is hard to let go of my past and forgive myself. It can be a process. What happens is that we often go looking for the "book" and dig it up again, and then we have to let it go again. Then we go down to the incinerator and dig through the ashes and get the book again, and then we have to give it up again. The letting-go on a human experiential level is often a process. You can read in the book of Psalms about the struggles of David in the midst of sin, and you find him writing several psalms in a row asking for the same thing—asking for God to forgive him. God forgave him the first time, but David was struggling with forgiving himself and with letting go.

6. *I suffer from post-traumatic stress syndrome and personality disorder. I often feel suicidal—at least once a week. Where can I find the faith to keep going? How can you trust when you're hurting so much? I believe God is there, but where?*

If you wrote this question tonight, why don't you come talk to David [a speaker during the service] afterward, because he is going through that struggle as well. Some of the deep struggles of life require not only help from God, but help from other people who are working through those struggles. It is not a sign of weakness to need help from somebody else. It is a very good and positive thing to do—to find a good Christian counselor to help you work through that struggle.

APPENDIX C

A LIST OF
"SATURDAY NIGHT" TOPICS

October 22—November 26, 1988

October 22	Why Is the Church Full of Hypocrites?
October 29	Would Jesus Be a TV Evangelist?
November 5	Is God a Democrat?
November 12	Is Religion for Wimps?
November 19	Would Jesus Wear a Rolex?
November 26	Sex?

January 28—August 5, 1989

January 14	Is Sex Really Free?
January 21	What Does the Bible Say About Divorce?
January 28	Are Singles Second-Class Citizens?
February 4	Marriage, Divorce, and Human Sexuality: An Open Forum
February 11	Christianity and Humanism
February 18	Christianity and Third-World Struggles
February 25	Christianity and Communism
March 4	Christianity and Satanism
March 11	Christianity and New Age
March 18	The Resurrection . . . Who Cares?
April 1	April Fools?
April 8	Why Am I Always Lonely?
April 15	If God Forgives Me, Why Can't I Forgive Myself?
April 22	Heaven and Hell . . . Myth or Reality?
April 29	Satanism . . . How Real Is It?
May 6	Can Love Be Rekindled?
May 13	Drugs and Alcohol . . . One Time Won't Hurt Me?
May 20	Am I a Work-a-Holic?
May 27	The Gay Community and the Church
June 3	Suicide . . . Do I Ever Think About It?
June 10	Death . . . Where Do I Go From Here?

April 14	God . . . Can He Be Trusted?
April 21	God . . . How Can I Know What He Wants Me to Do With My Life?
April 28	God . . . How Can I Get Him to Listen to Me?
May 5	Why Is the Bible the Only Right Book?
May 12	Child Abuse . . . It's a Killer . . . What Can I Do?
May 19	Adult Abuse . . . It's a Killer . . . What Can I Do?
May 26	Where Did You Get the Idea You Could Make It All by Yourself?
June 2	Hell . . . Fact or Fiction?
June 9	Heaven . . . Fact or Fiction?
June 16	Downtown . . . The Best of Saturday Night
June 23	Downtown . . . The Best of Saturday Night
July 7	On the Beach . . . (Grand Haven) . . . The Best of Saturday Night
July 14	On the Beach . . . (Grand Haven) . . . The Best of Saturday Night

October 6—December 1, 1990

October 6	Iraq and the Middle East . . . Is It the Beginning of the End?
October 13	If This Is the End of the World . . . How Much Time Is Left?
October 20	Scared to Death . . . How Can I Triumph Over Terror?
October 27	Sex . . . What's Love Got to Do With It?
November 3	Alone Again—Naturally! Is There Any Answer?
November 10	Bluer Than Blue—Sadder Than Sad . . . Is There Any Hope?
November 17	The Hurt Won't Go Away . . . Should I Get Mad or Get Even?
November 24	Who Can I Turn to, When Nobody Needs Me?
December 1	Reconciliation

January 5—July 13, 1991

January 5	"Shattered Dreams" (1) I'm Disillusioned, What Can I Do?
January 12	"Shattered Dreams" (2) How Can I Survive and Dream Again?
January 19	The Reality of War

June 15–22
(2 weeks)   "On the Road . . . Downtown" (Monroe Mall amphitheater)

July 6–13
(2 weeks)   "On the Road . . . Grand Haven" (Waterfront sta-
dium)

September 21—November 30, 1991

September 21   Love . . . What Is "Real" Love?
September 28   Love . . . How Can I Learn to Love Myself?
October 5   Love . . . Can I Ever Have "Real" Love for Others?
October 12   Love . . . Is It Possible to Experience God's Love for
Myself?

October 19   Trust . . . How Can I Begin to Trust?
October 26   Trust . . . How Can I Learn to Trust Myself?
November 2   Trust . . . Can God Be Trusted?
November 9   Suicide . . . What Does the Bible Have to Say?
November 16   How Can I Find Real Meaning in Life? (For Myself)
November 23   How Can I Find Real Meaning in Life? (In Relation-
ships)
November 30   How Can I Find Real Meaning in Life? (With God)

1992

January 4   Starting Over . . . How Can I After a Broken
Relationship?
January 11   Starting Over . . . How Can I After Great Personal
Loss?
January 18   Starting Over . . . How Can I After All My Failures?
January 25   Starting Over . . . Can God Give Me a Second
Chance?
February 1   A Christian . . . Isn't It Anyone Who Believes in
God?
February 8   A Christian . . . What Are They and What Do They
Believe?
February 15   A Christian . . . Aren't All Religions About the
Same?
February 22   A Christian . . . What's the Commitment and Life-
style?
February 29   Everything You've Always Wanted to Know . . . But
Were Afraid to Ask?

APPENDIX D

"SINGLES VIEWPOINT" TOPICS

September 21   Chivalry, Chauvinism, and Women's Lib: Who Pays for the Date?
September 28   Dating or Mating: How to Keep Communication Open and Honest
October 5   Still Single? What Seems to Be the Problem?
October 19   Dating Part II: Men Women Love/Men Women Leave
October 26   Single Adult Purpose: White Picket Fence or Name on the Door?
November 2   Celibacy or Marriage: Finding Mr./Mrs. "Right"
November 9   Addiction Part I: Alcohol 1, 2, 3 or More? (AA)
November 16   Addiction Part II: Alcohol 1, 2, 3 or More (Medical Data)
November 23   Addiction Part III: Sexual Addiction, What Is It?
November 30   Abortion: Murder or Choice?

Winter 1992

January 4   What's Life Like Being 6 Years Old?
January 11   What's Life Like Being 16 Years Old?
January 18   What's Life Like Being Different?
January 25   Single Adult Life: Good Date or Good Grief?
February 1   Single Adult Life: Communicating for Life
February 8   Single Adult Life: Money Matters
February 15   Is There Life . . . After Divorce?
February 22   Is There Life . . . After Getting Dumped?
February 29   Is There Life . . . After Losing Your Job?
March 7   Is There Life . . . After Age 65?
March 14   Asking the Experts . . . Attorneys
March 21   Asking the Experts . . . Doctors
March 28   Asking the Experts . . . Economists
April 4   Asking the Experts . . . Psychologists, Part I
April 11   Asking the Experts . . . Psychologists, Part II

Fall 1992

APPENDIX E

"SATURDAY NIGHT" SURVEY

Published March 17, 1992
Surveys taken January 12, 19, 26 in 1991 and January 11, 18, 25 in 1992

Points to remember:

> Most respondents do not answer every question.
> Many respondents give multiple answers for some questions.
> Survey covered the same three weeks of each calendar year.
> 36% (633) of the people present participated in the surveys.
> People were asked to complete only one questionnaire so that there would be no duplicate entries.
> Most percentages are rounded off to the nearest whole point.

The Preface
Total attendance during the three weeks of the survey:
  1991: 1,509 (avg. 503 per week)
  1992: 1,760 (avg. 587 per week)
  (Approximately 17% higher average attendance in 1992. The 1993 attendance is significantly higher.)

Number of persons responding to survey week by week:
  1991: 351 first week, 308 second, 261 third = 920 total
  1992: 397 first week, 147 second, 86 third = 630 total
  (Calvary Church has separate data for each week, but this summary combines the totals for the three weeks.)

154

The Survey

1. Do you attend church regularly (3 times a month)?

Year	Total	Number Yes	% Yes	Number No	% No
1991:	870	748	86.0	122	14.0
1992:	623	217	35.0	406	65.0

2. Do you attend Calvary Church?

Year	Total	Number Yes	% Yes	Number No	% No
1991:	873	444	51.0	429	49.0
1992:	626	277	44.0	349	56.0

3. How did you hear about "Saturday Night"?
(Most respondents gave more than one answer.)

Year	Total	R	BB	NP	F	O/C
1991:	902	63	86	122	363	268
		7%	9.5%	13.5%	40%	30%
1992:	709	46	77	81	355	150
		6.5%	11%	11.5%	50%	21%

Key = Radio, BillBoards, NewsPaper, Friends, Other/Church

Total media/advertising response: 1991 = 30%
1992 = 29%

4. Age Groups Present?

Year	Under 18	18–22	23–29	30–39	40+
1990:	55	122	203	139	104
	9%	20%	33%	23%	16%
1991:	39	121	216	213	219
	5%	15%	27%	27%	27%
1992:	17	61	166	200	188
	2.5%	10%	26%	32%	30%

Percentage of persons under age 30:
1990: 63% (380 out of 623)
1991: 46.5% (376 out of 808)
1992: 38.6% (244 out of 632)

5. **What is your favorite part of the program?**

Year	Total	ME	MU	DR	QA
1991:	891	215	172	168	159
		24%	19%	19%	18%
1992:	615	256	156	100	113
		42%	25%	16%	18%

Key = Message, Music, Drama, Question and Answer

47 people (8%) gave other responses: "all good," casual feel, friendly atmosphere, and testimonies.

6. **What is your least favorite part of the program?**

	All Good		Drama		Music	
Total	Number	%	Number	%	Number	%
234	120	51.0	66	28.0	21	8.0

At least 20 items were mentioned from the opening to the closing. The only ones that received significant mention were tabulated as shown. Of them, 28 thought the drama openings were "silly"; 18 thought the music was "too loud."

7. **If you could change "one thing" about "Saturday Night," what would it be?**

223 responses:
   "Change nothing": 101 (45%)
   "Music too loud": 34 (15%)
   "More time for Q & A": 26 (12%)
   "More music": 20 (9%)

Other responses from
   "The preacher's jeans" to "the comic scenes"
   The music "rock" to a drama "knock"
   "Why the time squeeze?" to "no offerings, please"

8. **Anything else you would like to say?**

450 responses said, "It's great! Keep up the good work!"

The Summary
   ● Attendance is up 17% (an aveage of 87 per night) from 1991 to 1992.

- The percentage of the persons in the age group of 30 years and older has increased by 23% as a part of the whole in the years 1990 to 1992.
- As many as 65% may be unchurched people on any given Saturday.
- Fewer Calvary people are attending than earlier (7% fewer in 1992 than in 1991).
- Media promotion is responsible for 29% who attend.
- "Singles Viewpoint" draws 125+ persons each week.
- We have 40+ "Ditch Digger" prayer partners. (Is it any wonder that this is the best year ever for "Saturday Night"?)
- The more mature audience is providing a greater stability and base for future growth than we have had before.
- We have given birth to three "new" Bible studies from the 1992 "Saturday Night."
- The "Greenhouse" Sunday school class is composed of mostly "Saturday Night" people.